Bedtime Story

Bedtime Story

A Play

Kiran Nagarkar

FOURTH ESTATE • *New Delhi*

First published in India in 2015 by Fourth Estate
An imprint of HarperCollins *Publishers*

Building 10, Tower A, 4th Floor, DLF Cyber City, Phase II,
Gurugram Haryana – 122002, India
www.harpercollins.co.in

P-ISBN: 978-93-5136-999-8
E-ISBN: 978-93-5177-000-8

2 4 6 8 10 9 7 5 3 1

Typeset in 11/14 Adobe Garamond Pro at
SURYA

Printed and bound at
MicroPrints India, New Delhi

INTRODUCTION

Is there such a thing as an apposite time, place or reason why a play, painting, symphony, or any other work of art is conceived? Perhaps there is, but I suspect it's comprehended mostly in retrospect. Looking back, I think I owe *Bedtime Story* to several factors coming together to jolt me out of my complacency and ignorance.

Let me try and record a few of them. Not many foreign magazines were available in India in the 1960s and '70s. In any case, I couldn't have afforded even the few that were. What I got to read were *Time* and *Newsweek*, and these were outdated office copies which one of the top managers left behind at the agency I worked for back then. You couldn't have found a better, or rather, a more uncritical reader than I was. Having been brought up in an old-school notion of journalistic values, I implicitly believed most of what I read in newspapers. The Vietnam War was progressing at a good clip, the Cultural Revolution in China was in full flood, and America was busy doing what it does so well, heroically fighting that handy bogey called communism on every front, never mind if the battlefront was thousands of miles away in Vietnam.

Then by chance I happened to read three biographies. The first one was about Henry Luce, the man primarily responsible for creating the *Time-Life* publishing empire and who was often referred to as the most influential private citizen of his time in America. Let me just say it was an eye-opener and leave it to your imagination to gauge how much of an understatement that is.

What I learnt was that the central principles of journalism—report what you see and not what you want to see; and, to the extent humanly possible, be objective—were consciously and repeatedly flouted by the boss-man at *Time* and *Life*. No, even that does not do justice to the man. Luce, for instance, had no qualms ignoring crucial reports on Chiang Kai-shek filed by Theodore White, one of his most respected journalists, and replacing them with completely fabricated reportage. Nothing that showed a Marxist regime in a favourable light, however factual it may have been, was tolerated.

It would, however, be foolhardy to think that much has changed since then. Newspapers and TV channels lie as glibly today as they did then and routinely suppress any point of view that differs from theirs. For instance, most American TV channels insisted that Israel had every right to bomb Gaza off the map in mid-2014 since Hamas had fired hundreds of rockets (which incidentally hardly hit any Israeli target), and that it was America's sacred duty to keep arming Israel. It was naturally of no consequence that, for years, Gaza has been an open prison that no Gazan can leave without Israeli permission. Gazans cannot conduct any business, cannot fish beyond three miles from their coastline, cannot import any food on their own, cannot have an airport or a port of their own, and cannot import urgently required medicines, or machines to start industries without Israeli permission.

By sheer accident, I ended up reading the Luce biography along with those of Ho Chi Minh and Fidel Castro, which I'd picked up on a visit to Strand Book Stall. I was far too caught up in the hand-to-mouth business of making a living, and given my lack of access to international news, had only vague notions about the history of Vietnam or its elections. No wonder it came as a surprise to me that the French, who had been ruling Vietnam long distance, had been forced to vacate the country by local freedom fighters after a gruesome war. But the real shock was to find that Ho Chi Minh had been democratically elected. And that the mother of all modern-day democracies, the USA, had decided that this tiny, newly independent country thousands of miles away was a threat to its existence and sovereignty and began to attack it. My ignorance was truly staggering.

Fidel Castro and Cuba were the next lessons in my political

education. I had vaguely heard of President Batista but it was news to me that this corrupt dictator was an American stooge and his regime, a nightmare. I learnt how Fidel Castro, Che Guevara, and a small band of fighters had ousted President Batista using a combination of courage, resolve and sheer happenstance or luck. Fidel and Che were avowed Marxists, a crime in the eyes of free-marketers, but they were liberators of their people from a venal and blood-sucking regime remote-controlled by its neighbouring superpower. I have little doubt that if America had not been so aggressively hostile, and had not repeatedly made attempts to overthrow Castro, and instead treated Cuba fairly, the communist dictatorship may have turned into a democracy in good time. Even as I write, President Obama has done a volte-face and relations between the US and Cuba have been normalized after over fifty years.

The Writing of *Bedtime Story*

I owe *Bedtime Story* to the rather belated but traumatic loss of my naiveté. I used to work in advertising, a profession that has been pilloried for lying, bamboozling and conning people. Journalism and scholarly research, on the other hand, were lauded for their probity, integrity and honest reporting. Now the scales had fallen off my eyes, at least superficially, since it's impossible to avoid the insidious and round-the-clock onslaught of various media and their owners' private agendas. But at least I had woken up to my own callousness towards the terrible injustices perpetrated around me. In truth, I had also become conscious of the fact that there is something worse than callousness, an outburst of righteous rage which subsides just as easily as it had risen.

My ruminations crystallized into a personal notion of responsibility and accountability, which would become, over the years, one of my basic tenets for practising that business called life. It was in this spirit that I began to write my first play, *Bedtime Story*. Let me say at the outset that I am at heart a Philistine and hold the view that the literary and the commercial are not mutually exclusive. I wish to entertain my readers or audiences (and not necessarily by writing Georges Feydeau–

type farces though I enjoy those hugely too), stimulate their minds, and, if possible, provoke them to introspect along with me. My role model has always been Samuel Taylor Coleridge's *Ancient Mariner* who catches hold of the wedding guest and keeps him in thrall, however reluctant a listener he may have been at the start. But I was also keen that any writing that tackled the issues that *Bedtime Story* set out shouldn't contravene my personal code: no overt messages and no preaching. If there was anything worthwhile in what I had to say, it would come through far more potently like a slow-release drug over weeks and months if the story was told powerfully and with conviction. Rightly or wrongly, I believed that the subterranean works better and one's concerns would automatically filter through.

My task was clear. Make the writing so compelling and hook the reader or the member of the audience from the word go so that he would only realize at the very end that passively watching the action unfold in *Bedtime Story* came at a heavy price. I chose to use stories from the Mahabharata as a medium to drive home my point about the malaise from which most of us suffer: apathy. (Incidentally I keep going back to this theme in much of my writing. In my novel *Cuckold*, the Maharaj Kumar remarks sardonically, 'With what fortitude we bear the misfortunes of others.') What I had going for me was the fact that the Mahabharata is a living epic in the subcontinent. It's in the bloodstream of almost every Indian—Hindu, Muslim, Christian or Buddhist. But I decided that I would ring unsettling changes in both the telling and in the stories themselves.

The theme of standing up and raising one's voice in protest and the appalling consequences of a 'what-can-we-do?' attitude gained urgency in 1975 when Indira Gandhi declared an Emergency in the country and abrogated the powers reposed in Parliament and the judiciary by appropriating all power to herself and her younger son.

I finished *Bedtime Story* some time in 1977. Emergency rule was terminated soon after and I thought my play had lost its sting. I couldn't have been more wrong. It was more pertinent at that moment than at any time before. Hardly anybody ever gets a second chance at life, especially when one realizes all too late how precious life is. But we Indians got a second chance because Mrs Gandhi made the biggest miscalculation of her career: she called for an election. The opposition had united under the banner of the Janata Party and won an astounding electoral victory. They came to power for the first time at the Centre. Instead of making good on their promises and showing the people that the new government could make democracy work, they were hell-bent on squabbling amongst themselves about who should be prime minister and what punishment Mrs Gandhi should undergo for declaring the Emergency. Lo and behold, Mrs Gandhi was back in power within three years.

What I had grasped and wanted to communicate to my audience was that if we don't take cognizance of the malpractices, the desecration of the Constitution and fundamental human rights, the brutality, violence, prejudice, hatred and the demagogic persecution of minorities wherever they occur in the world, take a stand and make our voices heard, we are squarely responsible for the consequences of our inaction. As Hedy Epstein, the outspoken ninety-year-old Jewish political activist said after the appalling carnage visited by Israel on the Palestinians in 2014, 'Anyone who stands idly by becomes complicit in what is going on.'

We Don't Give a Damn

I recall a woman from Iraq whose home had been bombed and her entire family killed. She was distraught and desperately seeking help from the American TV crew covering the incident. She stopped suddenly in the middle of a sentence and asked, 'Why am I talking to you? I know that neither you nor anyone else in the world gives a damn about what happens to us.'

She was right, of course. Nobody gave a damn. The TV crew had turned up by chance and she would make good breaking news. It's no different here in India or anywhere else. Hardly anyone of us gives a damn about what's happening in our country, or, for that matter, in front of our eyes. When some man in a Porsche or Mercedes gets out of his car on a crowded road and bashes a cyclist for not moving out of his way, we watch the spectacle with exemplary restraint. We manage to shrug off unforgiveable, headline-grabbing crimes like the premeditated grisly murders and persecution of thousands of Sikhs because a Sikh security guard killed Indira Gandhi in 1984. The justification we heard then was, 'When a big tree falls…' We have been persecuting, torturing and murdering Dalits for thousands of years and continue to do so with impeccable self-righteousness. Who can ignore the fact that the appalling Gujarat riots of 2002 raised the most troubling questions without providing genuine answers and a satisfactory closure that brought the criminals to justice.

Censorship and *Bedtime Story*

The actor and theatre director Dr Shreeram Lagoo was the first to try to stage *Bedtime Story*. He realized that the play was provocative and controversial material. He invited all the experimental theatre groups in Bombay for a reading in 1978 because he wanted the whole amateur theatre movement behind the play. In the meantime, the play had been sent to the censor board for certification, as the law in Maharashtra demands. It came back with seventy-eight cuts, some of them a page long, so that barely the jacket-covers were left. Eminent academics M.P. Rege, Pushpa Bhave, and a couple of others argued the case for *Bedtime Story* at a meeting of the censor board. Many of the excisions the board demanded were risible (e.g., drop the names of the Buddha, Mahatma Gandhi), some questions did not make any sense (e.g., why are you distorting the original myths?). I must admit I was hoping that the board would have at least some members from the Marathi literary elite who would have understood the thrust of the play. But I soon realized that I was deluding myself. The board was convinced that the play was a stain on our culture and needed to be severely sanitized.

There's an interesting footnote to the board meeting. As time elapsed and the clock ticked towards 1 p.m., the adamantine insistence on the cuts lost steam. We learnt later that many board members had travelled from other cities and all they wanted by then was the free lunch and their fees for having attended. When the director of the play finally got a letter from the board, the cuts had been reduced to twenty-four. But by then almost all the actors had withdrawn from the rehearsals because fundamentalist Hindu parties and organizations in Bombay, as it was known then, threatened the director, producer, actors and me, and even the very first rehearsal was not allowed to take place. It helped enormously that none of these vociferous guardians of our culture had read *Bedtime Story*.

Over the years several directors who felt strongly about the play tried to get it staged. Legal censorship in India can often be gauche, club-footed and hyper-protective of anything and everything but the freedoms of speech and expression. Extra-legal censorship in the country, however, is fearless and effective. It successfully prevented *Bedtime Story* from being performed for seventeen years.

Rekha Sabnis's theatre group, Abhivyakti, and the director Achyut Deshingkar kept faith with the play through all the turbulence it generated. They finally staged it in 1995. Experimental theatres run mostly on scarce funds and large doses of enthusiasm. What killed *Bedtime Story* after twenty-five performances was the absence of small, affordable theatres. The actors had such fun with the firecracker dialogue and the energy within the play and the difficult questions it raised that they pooled their money and revived the play two years later, this time in Hindi, and it had a few more performances. Sometime later, Vasant Nath staged the play in Cambridge, UK, and at the Fringe Festival in Edinburgh.

I have not been so lucky in publishing *Bedtime Story*. A prestigious and established publishing house offered to bring out the first edition of the play on four different occasions. Each time, a week or two before the contract was to be signed the publisher got cold feet and withdrew the offer.

This is the first time *Bedtime Story* is seeing the light of day in print. In the performed version, for the sake of brevity and impact, we had excised all the modern episodes that served as a counterpoint to the reinterpreted original stories. What you are about to read now is the original version in full.

The End-game

I am about to make an extraordinary and a seemingly self-aggrandizing claim that is likely to put off almost all readers. I have mentioned how *Bedtime Story* had become all the more germane in the immediate post-Emergency era. I had, however, not the vaguest idea then that the world would change so radically for the worse over the next few decades that it would make the theme of *Bedtime Story* even more pressing and relevant. At the same time, let me also state emphatically that nothing would make me happier than to find that the world had woken up to the multiple crises facing us and taken effective action, making my play irrelevant.

The crises I am referring to are of two varieties, both of an urgency mankind has never experienced before. The first is the legacy of military adventurism of the two feuding giants, the US and Russia, which started wars in different parts of the world such as Afghanistan and Iraq, armed sections of the populace and left behind vast arsenals of deadly weapons and munitions, which have come to haunt the benighted local citizenry. But it is the unintended offshoots of these temporary occupations that have given birth to the most dangerous groups of terrorists in the world. As you may have guessed, I am referring here not only to barbaric organizations such as Al-Qaeda and Boko Haram, but especially to ISIS or the Islamic State, which has taken torture, sadism and brutality to unimaginably fiendish levels.[1] Never before has the world seen so many refugees driven away from their homes. Millions have been displaced, resulting in horrendous suffering and hardship, and the UN is unable to cope with the sheer numbers and their demands for help and succour.

---

[1]Now we have also learnt that the CIA under the aegis of President Bush and all the President's men practised torture and demonic brutality against prisoners in Afghanistan, Iraq and in America itself that would compare with that of the ISIS, except the appalling beheading.

And yet even the ISIS threat pales into insignificance when compared with the calamitous state of the planet due to the climate crisis. Entire chunks of Bangladesh, Philippines, and scores of other countries are going to disappear in the next few years. National leaders around the world have known for years what the human race is up against. The apocalyptic consequences of our fossil fuel economies and unbridled consumerism are no longer in the realm of a celluloid dystopian fantasy—they are already here. The planet is witnessing unprecedented rises in temperatures, droughts, floods, typhoons, tornadoes, famines, the melting of the ice-cap on both poles, and the death and disappearance of thousands of animal, bird and water species. California is facing its worst drought in two thousand years. And as usual, it is the poor who are suffering the most.

What is incomprehensible is that even at this eleventh hour, leaders and power-brokers of the world are in denial. They are busy playing with words, engaging in double-talk, and sabotaging the initiatives necessary to avoid the death and suffering of large swathes of humankind. Even the most powerful and financially secure nations know damn well that they cannot escape to another planet. What is even worse is the pussyfooting insistence that the other party take action first.

Now, it's entirely true that developed nations have plundered the earth and its resources for God knows how many scores of years, fouling up the atmosphere in the process, and they should really pay the price for all the damage done. But as we all know there's no chance of that. On the other hand, like many developing nations, India's stance has been that it will take the urgent action required to reverse climate change later since it needs to develop its own economy first. Do the nations of the world really believe that this is a game of who blinks first? The time for the blame-game is long past. It's truly now or never for mankind.

The leaders of the developed nations and Wall Street and the fossil fuel industries are not going to get down to the urgent business of formulating a genuine and drastic timetable and stick to it unless we, the populations of the world, force them to, and are ourselves willing to make serious changes in our lifestyles.

No book, play or work of art can trigger changes overnight. *Bedtime Story* certainly can't. But it can, I hope, force people to wake up and think.

Kiran Nagarkar
Mumbai, December 2014

CHARACTERS FROM THE MAHABHARATA

The Pandavas

Dharmaraj: The eldest Pandava

Bheem: The second Pandava

Arjun: The third Pandava

Nakul and Sahadev: The two youngest Pandava brothers

Draupadi: Their wife

Kunti: Their mother

The Kauravas and their Allies

Suyodhan: The eldest Kaurava

Sushyasan: Suyodhan's brother

Shakuni: Their uncle

Gandhari: Mother of the Kauravas

Drona: The guru of both the hundred Kauravas and the Pandavas, and later, the commander-in-chief of the Kaurava forces

Munimji: Clerk

Karna: Illegitimate son of Kunti brought up by a charioteer and his wife; friend of the Kauravas and king of Angadesh

Others

Grandmother

Grandson

Ekalavya: A tribal chieftain

Present-day Characters

Chorus

Arjun: A high-caste medical student

Ekalavya: An 'untouchable' medical student

Father: Arjun's girlfriend's father

Brother: Arjun's girlfriend's brother

Bimal: Brother of the eldest son Raj

Arun: Brother of Raj

Rupali: Widow of Raj

Mother: Rupali's mother-in-law, mother of Raj

Salma: A woman from East Pakistan (now Bangladesh)

Allauddin: Salma's husband

Hell's angels

Soldiers from the Pakistani army

Soldiers from the Indian army and East Pakistani (Bangladeshi) resistance fighters

Suggestions for Division of Multiple Roles

1. Granny – Draupadi – Rupali – Salma – Gandhari
2. Ekalavya – Karna – sixth soldier
3. Drona – Shakuni
4. Father – Dharmaraj – first soldier
5. Brother – Krishna
6. Arjun – Arun – second soldier
7. Bheem – Bimal – third soldier
8. Nakul – fourth soldier
9. Sahadev – fifth soldier
10. Sushyasan – seventh soldier
11. Suyodhan – Allauddin
12. First man in audience – Munimji (clerk)
13. Four hell's angels – four gang members
14. Mother – woman in audience – Kunti's voice offstage

Single Roles

1. Chorus
2. Grandson
3. Second man in audience

Note: Nakul or Sahadev could also play the grandson

ACT 1, SCENE 1

(A bare stage. At the beginning of every scene, a man enters and hangs a placard on the right-hand side indicating the location of the new scene. It is central to the purpose of the play that almost every actor performs multiple roles. The actor who plays Ekalavya in the first act could play Karna in the second and third acts. The Grandmother, Draupadi and Gandhari should be played by the same woman. As far as possible, changes in costume, when required, should be made on the stage itself. For example, the Grandmother removes her wig and scarf, puts on a little make-up, and becomes a young woman.

If the audience is unfamiliar with the stories from the Mahabharata, distribute the three pages on background notes provided at the end of the play before the performance. Wherever necessary, update instances cited in the play to suit the times and the country where the play is performed. For instance, when the play was written, the list of multinationals included names like IBM, General Motors, Exxon, and other giant industrial empires. But as the fortunes of companies undergo changes one will have to replace them with the current almighty corporations. Needless to say, Facebook, Google or Amazon would take centre stage today.

Except in the modern scenes, the men are bare-chested. They wear light yellow silk dhotis, with a long scarf draped loosely around the neck or tied around the waist.

In the beginning, the Chorus stands on the stage in front of the curtain. Another option is to have the Chorus sitting on a low swing at the very edge of the stage. His legs touch the floor. Somewhere in the middle of his monologue, he begins to swing over the heads of the people in the first few rows, thereby violating the division between the stage and the audience.)

CHORUS

(Starts off somewhat falteringly, trying to gauge the mood of the audience. He is different from the usual playful, over-friendly chorus. He glances at the watch on his left hand)

I've been given five minutes. I've got to say everything I want to in that time. But I keep thinking that the curtain will go up or move sideways, or do something of the sort in exactly four minutes and forty-five seconds. And that cramps my style. I only want to make a couple of things clear. I want to assure you that this is a traditional play. You'll find conflict between good and evil here. Right is pitted against wrong in a battle that is familiar to all of us. In keeping with convention, good is scorned, insulted, brought to the edge of ruin. Base, sinful evil emerges victorious. You begin to wonder where in God's name God is. There seems to be no place for truth, humanity and righteousness in His world. But evil has used up all the rope there is, and God Himself descends upon the earth to destroy it. Truth triumphs in the end. There is jubilation everywhere and everyone lives happily ever after. So you see, this is a predictable play in a way. But I don't mean predictable in a derogatory sense. I'm certain it will live up to your wildest and most demanding expectations. All I'm saying is that the set-up here is friendly, familiar, safe. Nothing unexpected, shocking or exceptional is going to happen. In short, this is not an experimental or a new-wave play.

This is a stage, isn't it? Why am I standing on a stage? It's because the play is set squarely on the twin pillars of convention and tradition. In a conventional play, the stage and the auditorium never intermingle. Their respective places and roles are never reversed. Nobody claims that the audience is either responsible for or conniving at what happens on the stage. We on the stage are actors. Our business is to perform a play. You are the audience. You sit before us, but at a distance. And that is why our play remains a play. Distance. That's the keyword in theatre.

(A group of Hell's Angels gathers on the stage. They carry rubber-padded batons, motorbike chains and machine guns. Some patrol the auditorium

aisles on soft feet. A couple of them swing the chains menacingly over their heads.)

You are probably wondering what these armed men are doing here. Don't let them worry you. They are here to protect us. Some innocents amongst you might question why people would need protection in a theatre. Don't ask me this question please and make me rake up those unpleasant memories. You can't have already forgotten the stones on the first night of *Ghashiram Kotwal* or how they forced *The Last Temptation of Christ* to close down though it had been passed by the Censor Board. But you will see how safe we are going to be today. Nobody has the guts to spoil our evening with these Angels around.

(The curtain has been rising slowly during the last few seconds. On the extreme left of the stage, a white-haired old woman appears. She sits with her grandson's head on her lap. Her eyes are blindfolded. The Chorus glances quickly at his watch, feeling abashed.)

Oh hell. I've stretched my five minutes to seven. Mustn't hold things up.

(Exit. If the Chorus is on the swing, he gets off and exits. The swing is pulled up out of sight or tucked away to the side.)

GRANDMOTHER

(her voice could be either melodious, or toneless and scratchy)

Cradle of gold,
Shining silver cord.
Beautiful baby,
Gift of the Lord.
Dewdrop dreams
On sleep's breeze driven.
New star in the sky,
Child of heaven.

GRANDSON

Shan't sleep even if you sing to me. You said yesterday you'd tell me a story.

GRANDMOTHER

It's late, my pet. Sleep now, and I'll tell you a story tomorrow.

GRANDSON

No. You promised.

GRANDMOTHER

All right. All right. Once upon a time, there was a king named Pandu. He had five sons, Dharmaraj, Bheem, Arjun, Nakul and Sahadev. Pandu had a brother called Dhritarashtra. This brother had a hundred sons, and they were called the Kauravas. Suyodhan and Sushyasan were the two eldest Kauravas. When King Pandu died, Dhritarashtra ascended the throne. He sent the five Pandavas and the hundred Kauravas to school together. They had a teacher called Dronacharya. He taught them arithmetic, history, wrestling, riding, geography and archery.

(The spotlight shifts from the grandmother and her grandson to the centre of the stage where Dronacharya and his pupils are gathered. The scene indicator reads: 'An open field'.)

DRONACHARYA

You've really been living it up, haven't you? No classes for a week. And the film festival here to add to the fun. Suyodhan, how many films did you see? Twenty-eight at the rate of four a day, or was it thirty-five at five a day? And you, Arjun? Painting the town red the first half of the night, and whoring the rest? After all, it's a man's prerogative. But the jaunt is over. Old man work is back on our necks. Now Sushyasan, what was our last lesson about?

SUSHYASAN

You were dealing with the aesthetics of Parashuram's archery and the principles behind it. The greater the pull, you said, the longer the flight of the arrow. One must always define one's objective first. Does one want to kill or wound: on that depends one's aim and the degree of tension on the bowstring. Missing your target is not a crime. If you miss, you miss. But the further your arrow strays, the sharper a target you become for the god of death, Yama.

DRONA

Excellent, Sushyasan. Now before your next pulse beat, tell me what target has caught your eye?

SUSHYASAN

I see a never-ending field, and at the very edge of it, at the extreme limit of vision, I see a peepul tree.

DRONA

Suyodhan, tell me before you can blink your eyes, what target do you see before you?

SUYODHAN

I see a parrot in the topmost branches of the peepul tree.

DRONA

And what is your eye fixed on, Arjun?

ARJUN

On the dead centre of the parrot's eye.

DRONA

You have gone to the very heart of the matter, Arjun. Blessed is the guru who has so brilliant a student.

(Ekalavya appears from behind a bush and throws himself at Dronacharya's feet.)

DRONA

Your name?

EKALAVYA

One who seeks only your blessings.

DRONA

Your name?

EKALAVYA

One whose heart has held a single desire this past year.

DRONA
Your name?

EKALAVYA
One who dares to aspire to become your student. Ekalavya.

DRONA
Arise.

EKALAVYA
Your blessings, guru.

DRONA
And if I don't bless you?

EKALAVYA
I can but request.

DRONA
Let us see the face behind the request. *(Ekalavya stands up.)* Whose son are you?

EKALAVYA
Black Ekalavya. That is enough. The rest is history. For one constant year have I watched you and your gifted students. Never closing my eyes, like a vigilant god. Every second of every day I wanted to throw myself at your feet and every second, every day I lost heart. Until today, Arjun's answer gave me courage.

DRONA
I have been patient, boy. You have spoken much. Ten words when two would have done. But there are limits that you may not overstep. Arjun is a prince. Who are you to address him by his name?

EKALAVYA
I am Ekalavya, son of the earth and the future king of the tribe of Bhils. I am proud to call Arjun, the third Pandava, by his name.

DRONA
A Bhil, a Mahar, a leper. There's no place for subtle distinctions among untouchables.

EKALAVYA
Call me what you like. Make me do any kind of work. Keep me awake day and night. Make me clean up garbage, leftovers, shit. I am willing to serve all hundred Kauravas and the five Pandavas. Then, if you wish, I will be your slave forever.

DRONA
If I wish? Why, you are a slave as it is. I am letting you off lightly today because of your youth. But if you dare come before me again, I will sever your head from your body without a second thought. Remember that.

EKALAVYA
Is that your final word?

DRONA
It is.

EKALAVYA
If you change your mind, I will not hold it against you. *(Deeply offended, Drona is about to fly off the handle.)* Take your time, Dronacharya. Don't give me a rash answer in the heat of the moment. Arjun, is there anything you wish to say? Your skill is such that it adds lustre to your guru's teaching. Accept me as your student, and I will be forever grateful to you. Or make Dronacharya change his decision. In either case, you will find me beside you in your hour of direst need when I will gladly give up my life for you.

(Arjun shrinks away, shaking his head, partly scared, partly confused.)

ARJUN
Never, even if my life were at stake, would I offend my guru. And if another dares to, he would have to pay with his life.

EKALAVYA

Noble sentiments from a noble prince. So, I will have to pay with my life, will I?

ARJUN

Your sort never learn their lesson through persuasion. One day I will make you bite the dust. When, is an irrelevant question.

EKALAVYA

You've won this round, but there will be another. The sun will go into a sudden eclipse. In that premature twilight the distinction between reality and illusion will become blurred. The sky will change. Circumstances will change. And you will not even remember that we had met before. Honoured guru, I prostrate myself before you, but from a distance. Think kindly of your student.

ACT I, SCENE II

(The indicator reads: 'An open field'. Enter Ekalavya, running. Arjun trails behind.)

ARJUN

I can't, Ekalavya, I can't take another step.

EKALAVYA

Just a few miles more, Arjun, and we'll be safe. We've lost them now, but if we waste any time, they'll be breathing down our necks again.

ARJUN

I'm through. *(Flops on the ground.)*

EKALAVYA

Get up. If we give up now, we're lost.

ARJUN

Not we, only I. Why you insist on running away with me when you've committed no crime, is something only you and your God know.

EKALAVYA

Come, get up. While we have feet, we have a way. And while there's a way, there's a chance of escape.

ARJUN

Damn you, I won't get up. They'll have to come and hoist me up.

EKALAVYA

Those people are insane, Arjun. They're not going to stand around arguing with you. All they want is murder. A few more months and we'll be full-fledged doctors. No one will touch us then. Come on, let's run. Give me your hand. We can relax once we're in the Mahar colony. Nobody will dream of looking for you there.

ARJUN

Why should I run like a criminal? I've done nothing wrong. I've been sleeping with Draupadi for the last two years. Only this time we got caught. Draupadi thought that the whole family had gone off to see *Gone with the Wind*. Blessed freedom for three hours. *(Laughs.)*

EKALAVYA

Shut up and come on. Those people will catch up with us any moment now.

ARJUN

(ignoring him) You should have seen her old man. He'd hurried back because he'd forgotten the tickets at home. We didn't hear him when he opened the door. All that frantic fornication tends to make one deaf. He watched us speechless. It was only when he planted a real scorcher on my arse that I jumped up, startled, gathered my clothes and ran. Draupadi's mother and brother must be still waiting for the tickets.

EKALAVYA

Like hell. The brother and his gang are leading the chase. If he gets his hands on you, there won't be time for your funny stories. He'll just feel high-minded and beat the shit out of you.

ARJUN

Let him do what he wants. I'm staying put. My morals are for saving my patients, Ek. They've got nothing to do with my sleeping with Draupadi. If you don't understand this simple difference you are dumber than you look.

EKALAVYA

And if you don't understand when to run for your life and when to make a stand, there's not much to choose between you and Draupadi's people.

ARJUN

Fine. Then go ahead and join them.

EKALAVYA

(shakes Arjun by the shoulders) You fool. Do you know what it means to be a doctor? God, how shall I tell you?

ARJUN

You don't have to. I'm studying medicine too, you know.

EKALAVYA

But that's the whole point. In my village when an old cow or ox died, someone would come over and holler to one of us untouchables, 'Hey you, come and collect the carcass.' I was seven when my mother got food poisoning eating such a cow. She vomited for two days and I settled down patiently waiting for her to die. But she didn't die. Not that time anyway. Somebody got hold of a doctor from the Christian mission. My mother lived. And so did the doctor, in my heart.

ARJUN

Very inspiring. Save it for your autobiography.

EKALAVYA

We have a job to do, Arjun. We have to save my mother, my mother's mother, and my mother's grandmother. Come with me. Run man, run.

ARJUN

I won't. Not with you anyway.

EKALAVYA

Why? What's stopping you? My bloody untouchability?

ARJUN

Maybe. You're a responsibility I can't cope with, Ek. If you're caught with me and are forced to give up your medical studies, I'll never forgive myself.

EKALAVYA
They're after you, not me. Whatever the allegation, whether true or false, it's against you, not me.

ARJUN
You and your romantic notions. Every time you save a man or a child you hope that sometime, somewhere, he'll remember, and treat one of your people like a human being. But get this straight, if ever one of us is to be sacrificed, there's no doubt who it will be.

EKALAVYA
Damn it, Arjun, can't you see that I can't afford to have you caught? Because without you, your people will remain Draupadi's father and brother, and without me, my people will remain Mahars. Someone has to start a new generation, start being human, decent, just. Now run, Arjun, run.

(Ekalavya runs to the edge of the wings. Draupadi's father, brother and his gang surround Arjun.)

FATHER
Your time's up, Arjun. We've got you now.

(*They attack Arjun. His screams grow fainter. Ekalavya steps forward.*)

EKALAVYA
You'll kill him if you beat him anymore.

(They stop.)

BROTHER
That's the untouchable bastard from the medical college. Some guts he's got, talking to us like that. You lowdown scum of the earth, you. You think you can step off the dunghill on which you were born, come into our town and rape our women?

(They're about to attack him with knives and daggers when Draupadi's father intervenes.)

FATHER

Stop it. Enough is enough. First it was that do-gooder Mahatma Gandhi who filled their heads with ideas. Then came our spineless government, reserving all the best jobs for them. They're Mahars when it suits them. Otherwise they're Neo-Buddhists. They're getting too smart by half, the bastards. No. He's not going to die this easy. We are still full-blooded men, thank the Lord.

(They gag Ekalavya and tie up his hands and feet. One or two sit on his arms and legs while someone undoes his trouser buttons.)

BROTHER

Crush his balls. Let's castrate the whole tribe. No Mahar is ever going to lay his hands on our girls.

(They ungag Ekalavya. All this time Arjun has been sitting nearby, shaking his head in disbelief and fear. Having castrated Ekalavya, Draupadi's father and the others glance at Arjun and exit.)

EKALAVYA

Arjun, Arjun…

(Arjun shudders. Still shaking his head, he follows the others out.)

ACT I, SCENE III

(The indicator reads: 'An ancient jungle'. Dronacharya is with his pupils.)

SUSHYASAN
Did you see that, Arjun? What a fantastic musk-deer.

ARJUN
Was it real? Or an apparition?

SUYODHAN
How pleased Mother will be if we capture it for her.

DRONA
You want it alive, don't you? What's stopping you then? Take it. It's your kingdom.

ARJUN
How? It disappeared almost before we saw it.

DRONA
What are those deadly hounds for, if not to give chase? Arjun, order them to surround the deer without harming a hair on its body. We'll follow.

(The ferocious barking of dogs is heard offstage.)

SUYODHAN
They're off, swift as arrows. I'm glad they're ours. I'd hate to fall foul of them.

(Suddenly the dogs stop barking.)

ARJUN
They've got the deer already. Truly, the hound is the only dog worth having. Let's go and claim our deer.

DRONA
Don't be a fool. I smell danger. The dogs have been killed, or something terrible has happened to them. We must be wary.

SUYODHAN
How suddenly the sun has been eclipsed. I can't believe my eyes. The deer's nowhere in sight. And yet the dogs stand there petrified, a single arrow holding them at bay.

BHEEM
Who dares hold our hounds to ransom? Let me get rid of the arrow and then I'll show the bastard. *(He makes a move to rush into the wings.)*

DRONA
Don't move, anybody. There has been enough foolishness for one day. Arjun, set those hounds free with one of your special missiles.

(Arjun fixes an arrow to his bow and sends it flying. Everybody looks surprised, and then, with the exception of Dronacharya, they all burst out laughing. Arjun looks mortified.)

SUYODHAN
Well, well, Arjunrao. The greatest archer's arrows have become powerless, have they?

SUSHYASAN
Cheer up cousin. With a little bit of luck you'll be doing worse than that.

DRONA
Silence. Our lives are in danger. This is no time for mockery.

(Enter Ekalavya.)

EKALAVYA
Stop chasing my deer and your hounds will be freed.

ARJUN
We are princes. This kingdom is ours. Its people are ours. Geography is ours. History is ours. The air is ours. You are ours. The deer is ours.

EKALAVYA
Take it if it's yours.

DRONA
Don't take what Arjun says to heart. He is young. Like you. And he doesn't know when to give in. Who do I have the pleasure of…

ARJUN
(interrupting angrily, but only loud enough for Drona's ears) Give in? I? When you'd promised that nobody else on earth would be my equal in archery?

DRONA
Who are you?

EKALAVYA
The deer is mine.

DRONA
Yes, of course. The deer is yours. Arjun, it is not right for a prince to covet his people's property. Who are you?

EKALAVYA
Black Ekalavya. And your student, Dronacharya, I prostrate myself at your feet. You asked me my name as a mere formality. But you knew who I was, didn't you?

DRONA
Don't we always know?

ARJUN
(a little louder than before) But you had promised.

DRONA
Promises must subserve circumstance, Arjun. The man who comes to terms with reality is a wise man. *(To Ekalavya.)* I have never seen such

fantastic archery in my life. Praise be to your guru. He is a fortunate man indeed to have so gifted a student.

EKALAVYA

We have the same guru, Dronacharya, your pupils and I. Look, there he is. Take a good look at him. *(Ekalavya points to a small image of Dronacharya.)* Every single day for the last five years, I prostrated myself before your image and asked for your blessings. Then in that total non-light, where no bird stirred, where there was neither moon nor starlight, where no candle was lit, where the sun itself could not pierce the green-black denseness of the jungle, I practised.

DRONA

It is a fantastic tale. I would not have believed such skill was possible had I not seen it with my own eyes. Imagine what feats you would have performed had you trained under me instead of my image.

EKALAVYA

You had the opportunity Dronacharya, but you spurned it.

DRONA

How true, how true.

ARJUN

(louder and more insistent this time) Dronacharya, how often must I remind you of your promise that I would be the finest archer in the world?

DRONA

So you will, you will. Truly, Ekalavya, I have no words with which to praise you. What you achieve with your bow lies beyond the imagination of man. I feel fulfilled with the faith you have shown in me. I must go now. But not without honouring you by accepting a gift from you, your gurudakshina.

EKALAVYA

That is your right and my privilege.

DRONA

Just a small remembrance, Ekalavya, a mere token.

EKALAVYA

Command me, Dronacharya.

DRONA

Are you sure you will not refuse?

EKALAVYA

You have no reason to doubt me.

DRONA

That is true. But if you refuse I will not be able to tolerate the insult. Because it will be an insult to the most deeply cherished and honoured tradition of our culture, the guru–shishya relationship. It is through this tradition that knowledge, virtue and religion are perpetuated.

EKALAVYA

You have only to ask, Dronacharya. Ask without hesitation.

DRONA

All right then. A small gift, Ekalavya. The thumb of your right hand.

(Nobody can believe his ears. Even Arjun's mouth falls open in shock. Only Ekalavya's expression remains unchanged.)

EKALAVYA

So be it.

(He bends down, picks up a little earth, spits in it, moulds it into the shape of a thumb, places it on a leaf, goes down on his knees and offers it to Dronacharya in cupped hands.)

EKALAVYA

Like guru, like gift. *(Pauses.)* Do you remember my words, Arjun? 'The sun will go into a sudden eclipse. In the premature twilight, the distinction between reality and illusion will be blurred. The sky will change. Circumstances will change. And you will not even remember that we had met before.' Be on your guard, Arjun. Beware the guru who discriminates between one student and another. Excellence comes through competition with one's betters. Beware the guru who will betray you in your hour of direst need and join the enemy against you.

(Fade out.)

CHORUS

Didn't I tell you a little while ago that distance is the keyword in theatre? Are you convinced now? There's no telling how people on the stage will behave. Strange, perverse people. Did you see how they were after Arjun's blood at first, and then suddenly turned on Ekalavya? That sort of thing never happens in our lives. Getting back to our own little world is a blessed relief after a play like this. Not meddling in other people's affairs, just carrying on with our little jealousies and getting the kids married off, and tea with friends, and a newspaper in the morning. Once in a while there's news that a couple of tribals' eyes have been gouged out, or their huts burned down, or their lands snatched away. But those are exceptions. And anyway who can say how much truth there is in such reports and how much is rumour.

Sometime ago I went to see *The Diary of Anne Frank*. What a play. I'm sure you've seen it too. How I wept. I identified with Anne so completely, she and I became one. What courage that girl had, what faith in humanity. When I came out, my heart was deeply stirred. My spirit soared. I felt as uplifted as I had felt years ago, listening to the Führer's speeches against the Jews, and crying out Heil Hitler! How can I forget those marvellous, halcyon days of my youth? Starched brown shirts and starched brown shorts with the oblique swastika on the sleeve. Oh, it was wonderful to be alive then, with all that power and blond camaraderie surging around you.

After the play, I lingered on the steps, still in the clouds. Somebody near me said, 'What monsters those Nazis must have been. Look at the way they tortured that tender, innocent girl.' I threw a glance at the speaker from my heady, rarefied heights, and suddenly it came back to me. It was the same face. I could never forget it. My Nazi comrades and I were escorting a handcuffed Anne down the stairs when a mouse-like face peeped out at us and disappeared back into its hole. It was a scared face, a little happy that others were suffering, a little grateful to God that he had escaped the same fate. An undistinguished, ordinary sort of face. Exactly like millions of other faces. Etched into my memory with a laser.

What a play! Everybody can identify with Anne Frank. How comfortable it makes us all feel. If all of us are Anne Franks, maybe there weren't any Nazis or, for that matter, Nazi supporters. Maybe they were just a figment of our imagination. Why don't we have more plays like that, honestly? So that Stalin's purges, the Partition massacres, the thousands of women, children and old men starving in Somalia, the ethnic cleansing in Bosnia can be obliterated forever.

(The spotlight focuses on the Grandmother.)

GRANDMOTHER

Do you know what happened then? The five Pandavas and the hundred Kauravas and Karna and many other kings and princes went to the kingdom of Panchal to vie with each other for Princess Draupadi's hand.

ACT II, SCENE I

(The indicator reads, 'The State of Panchal: Draupadi's Wedding'. The Grandmother removes her wig and scarf and makes herself up as Draupadi. A shining cauldron stands centre stage. A fish hangs above it but almost out of sight. The Pandavas stand to the left of the cauldron, the Kauravas and Karna to the right. Beyond the cauldron stands Draupadi.)

NAKUL

No, that's not fair. You're not allowed to peep at the target through the corner of your eye. King Panchal said so. We're supposed to look at the reflection in the cauldron and shoot through the fish's eye. No cheating please.

SUYODHAN

Oh shut up. Let Sushyasan concentrate, can't you?

BHEEM

Why? You don't want him to win, do you?

SUYODHAN

As long as the Pandavas don't get Draupadi, I don't care who does—Sushyasan or my other brothers or Karna or I.

NAKUL AND SAHADEV

(laughing heartily when Sushyasan misses the target) Ho, ho, ho. What happened? Was it a cramp in the hand or a cataract in the eye?

SUSHYASAN

Let's see what you can do, you jokers.

NAKUL

Be my guest. Here I fix my arrow and here...

SUYODHAN

And here you miss. Run along now and send your Siamese twin. Or better still, advise him to make himself scarce. He'll only make a fool of himself.

(Sahadev pushes his sleeve up and accidently drops his arrow in the cauldron. Laughter. Suyodhan snatches the bow from him and assumes several postures. Finally he misses.)

BHEEM

That's it, cousin. Low angle, long shot, close up, pan, zoom and … missed. The tools are bad they say. And the target's all wrong. Suyodhan, accept my heartfelt condolences.

SUSHYASAN

Oh mother of King Kong and son of Gargantua, come on then, show us what you can do.

BHEEM

I'll show you, all right. Just hop into the arena and watch how I make mincemeat of you.

SUYODHAN

This is no wrestling match, friend. That's in Kolhapur tomorrow. You've come to the wrong place. This, in case it's escaped you, is a swayamwar. So you just give that arrow of yours an aeroplane spin, drop kick and neck chop … oops! Not half as bad as it might have been. Cheer up. At least you got the fish's tail if not the eye.

SUSHYASAN

(in a low voice) Come on, Karna. The honour of the Kauravas is at stake. Here's your chance to avenge yourself on those who insulted you by not admitting you to the Olympics.

DRAUPADI

Put that bow down and declare who you are.

KARNA

I am Karna, future king of Angadesh.

DRAUPADI

Only by law and by favour of the Kauravas. By birth you are the son of a charioteer. A borrowed kingdom does not give you the right to compete for my hand. Assembled here today are the kings and princes of a hundred countries. If you do not wish to be humiliated before them, I'd advise you to go and hide behind your benefactors.

(Karna, Sushyasan and Suyodhan angrily prepare to leave. Just then Arjun's arrow pierces the fish's eye dead centre. There's a burst of applause. Karna walks to Arjun. The audience grows suddenly still, expecting something untoward to happen. Draupadi, advancing with a garland, stands rooted to the spot.)

KARNA

That was a beautiful shot. I don't think I could have matched it. Draupadi is a fortunate woman.

(He leaves along with the other Kauravas. Draupadi garlands Arjun. He takes her hands in his.)

ARJUN

Draupadi, you don't have to marry me just because my arrow hit the target. Marry the man of your choice. Anybody in this hall on whom your heart is set. Even Karna.

DRAUPADI

One hundred and seventy times was the bowstring pulled, one hundred and seventy times were the arrows released, and one hundred and seventy times did I die in these two hours. Each time I prayed that the arrow might miss its mark and I be saved from marrying a man I did not desire. Then you picked up the bow and I forgot to pray. And now I am yours, Arjun, only yours. If somebody else's arrow had hit the target, I swear to you, Arjun, I would have stolen out of my husband's bed and lost my virginity to you.

ARJUN

Come then, Draupadi. You will never regret marrying me for a single moment of your life. *(Arjun gives Draupadi a long kiss.)* You said you almost died and your world collapsed into black holes of despair a hundred and seventy times. Let's make up for it now. Come, Draupadi, we'll invent the coiled double helix of life. Come, come, Draupadi. One hundred and seventy centuries await us, and time is running short. Dada, Bheem, Nakul, Sahadev, let's hurry home. Mother must welcome her daughter-in-law before the sun goes down.

(The Pandavas go round the stage. Backstage the sun comes to rest on the horizon.)

ARJUN

Mother, Mother, where are you, Mother? You will never guess, not in seven lifetimes, what a beautiful, beautiful gift I have brought you.

KUNTI

(offstage) Arjun dear, I haven't the patience to wait for seven lifetimes. Whatever it is that you have brought for me, share it with your brothers as usual.

(There's a paralysed silence. Draupadi waits for a minute and then smiles.)

DRAUPADI

Arjun, tell your Mother it isn't a new kingdom, or a chocolate cake that you've brought for her this time. Tell her it's a living woman who talks and laughs and is mad with joy, and belongs to you alone, and cannot be shared amongst the five of you.

ARJUN

(collapses on his knees in anguish) What have you done, Mother? What have you done?

(The same silence again. Draupadi begins to suspect there's something terribly wrong but she can't take the situation seriously yet.)

DRAUPADI

Arjun, stop playing games. Why can't you be plain with her? Nothing so terrible or irrevocable has happened that it can't be explained. Call her out. Let her see me. She knows as well as anyone that a woman is not an object for a man to possess but a human being in her own right, equal to him and happy to be his companion.

KUNTI

(offstage) Arjun, tell her I cannot come out today. It is my time of the month.

DRAUPADI

You need not come out. But you can at least take back your word.

DHARMARAJ

A mother's word is never withdrawn.

DRAUPADI

Who said so?

BHEEM

That's the rule of this house anyway.

DRAUPADI

Let's change our house, Arjun.

ARJUN

How can I go back on my mother's word?

DRAUPADI

For heaven's sake, Arjun, you can't tie yourself down for life to something she said through sheer misunderstanding. How soon you've forgotten this morning. You fixed your arrow to the bow and your sinews stood up hard and taut. Your left leg placed precisely eighteen inches ahead of your right, your body balanced upon your feet with such delicate sureness that an earthquake could not have shaken you. Your eyes focussed in effortless concentration. Never before had I set eyes on so perfect a man. Your arrow flew forth and, lost in ecstasy, I moved forward to touch you. I stumbled for a moment on the edge of the dais and came down to earth. My eyes met Karna's and I knew that he alone in that vast gathering had seen my soul stripped naked. The blood drained out of my face. Not with shame but from habit. Come,

Arjun. This morning's promise still waits impatiently for fulfillment. Give me your hand.

(Arjun moves forward to put his hand in hers. As their hands touch, his excited brothers react sharply.)

DHARMARAJ

Arjun, you no longer have sole right over her.

BHEEM

We are all partners.

NAKUL

Even small fry like us.

SAHADEV

And Draupadi is our capital.

DRAUPADI

You have all gone stark, raving mad. You're going to share me just because Mummy said so? And you expect me to turn myself into a five-day roster to please you? I'm supposed to divide myself into five portions? Listen to me, Arjun, and listen well. You won me in fair competition. Those four brothers of yours lost. If I stay here, I stay as your wife, not as the mistress of five brothers. Are you coming with me or aren't you?

ARJUN

I brought you here with such hopes and dreams, Draupadi. I humbled the Kauravas with your help. If anybody had dared to suggest that the daughter-in-law of the Pandava house would not get along with her mother-in-law, I would have slit his throat.

DRAUPADI

Then come and slit my throat, my dear, petticoated husband. Because that's just what I'm saying. I will never see eye to eye with that invisible mother of yours. Not in seven lifetimes.

DHARMARAJ

A mother's word is sacred. We are five brothers and there's not a trace of jealousy or envy amongst us. Not even in the legends will you find love to equal ours. The world will be dazzled by you and Arjun, the perfect couple. But when all five of us unite with you, the very heavens will gaze upon us wonderstruck. Sex is only the animal aspect of love. Man transcends the animal in him with the sublime fusion of souls.

DRAUPADI

(listening to him in disbelief) You can't be serious. I've never heard anybody talk such sanctimonious drivel and believe it. Your name is Dharma, isn't it? The guardian of truth and dharma? You are supposed to be the most truthful of all men. Then tell your brother that you don't have a ghost of a right over his wife.

DHARMARAJ

In accordance with the rules of swayamwar, we brothers have indeed no right over Arjun's wife. But truth is the slave of time. Today's truth is the sovereign truth. Mother spoke many hours after your swayamwar. What she says carries greater weight by virtue of time. And so I have the first right to enter your bed.

DRAUPADI

Mama's little pet, how much more wool are you going to pull over your eyes and mine? If you want me, say so. If you'd been honest about it, I might even have let you have me once, just once. Bheem, you have no intellectual pretensions. You don't torture words to turn black into white. You understand, don't you, that I am not your wife?

BHEEM

Mother said you belong to all of us.

DRAUPADI

(looks at Nakul and Sahadev and shudders) They are all alike, every single brother wants to sleep with me. But I'd rather drop dead than have anything to do with them. Listen to me, God, wherever you are. I lay my curse on Pandu's progeny. May the nectar of success always

turn to poison at their lips. May Kunti's sons be snatched away from her the way she has snatched my husband away from me.

DHARMARAJ

Careful, Draupadi. You, too, now belong to the house of Pandu.

DRAUPADI

I'm off. If I have to prostitute myself, why stop at five men? *(The Kauravas and Karna walk past in the background.)* Over there stand the hundred Kauravas, all lusting after me, with Karna thrown in as a bonus. *(Runs and accosts Karna.)* Karna, Karna, mine has been a terrible mistake. How I have wronged you. Don't forgive me, ever. Punish me every hour, but save me from these mealy-mouthed hypocrites. *(Karna's eyes are fixed on a distant spot. Draupadi grips his arms and shakes them violently.)* I can't bear this humiliation, Karna. How far I have travelled in these twelve hours … from a princess to a prostitute.

(Karna continues to look into the distance, but pulls Draupadi close to him and caresses her face with great tenderness.)

KARNA

How long is it since I saw you last? Ten years? Or was it fifteen, or fifty? You were young then. And I was in love with you. When I saw you for the first time in the marriage hall, something snapped violently within me. But snapping, it didn't break me. Only released me. So that when I breathed in, I felt the whole earth entering me, and when I breathed out it was as if the universe were rushing out of me. You were so pure and untouched by experience. You could have demanded anything of me and I would have grown in the fulfilment of each demand. I was ready to challenge the world on the strength of my tiny, borrowed kingdom. But it was morning then. And now it is ninety minutes since the sun went down.

DRAUPADI

Karna, I too have travelled as great a distance as the sun in that time. Take me with you and let us forget what happened today.

KARNA

(he hasn't heard her) It was morning then, and you were my first love. Now it is night. All you can give me now is what any two-bit slut off Foras Road could give. Let it be.

(Fade out.)

(Commotion in the front rows of the audience. A man's voice screams, 'Stop this vile, blasphemous play. Stop it.' Four of the Hell's Angels quickly go down. There are sounds of someone being beaten up. Suddenly, one of the Angels whips out a pistol and shoots four times. The auditorium freezes into total silence. Chorus enters.)

CHORUS

Okay, okay. Easy, everybody. Relax. Relax. There's no need to worry. We can't have a play without some commotion. Somebody out there was trying to be funny. But our friends here acted promptly and brought things under control.

(The blood-soaked body of the victim is carried out by the four Angels.)

ACT II, SCENE II

(The indicator reads, 'A penthouse in Bombay'. Bare stage as in the rest of the play.

Rupali, in a white sari, is sitting centre stage on a stool that's used in front of a dressing table. Her mother-in-law stands next to her. Rupali looks straight ahead as if she were scrutinizing her image in a mirror.)

RUPALI

(wiping the big bold circle of crimson powder at the centre of her forehead with the palm of her right hand) Happy? *(She yanks at the mangalsutra chain at her neck with force and lets it fall to the ground.)* Happy? *(Her mother-in-law comes forward, carrying a round silver plate. Rupali breaks her coloured glass bangles on the plate.)* Happy? We are even now, both of us widows, dispossessed and disabused of power. *(Mother-in-law turns her back and walks up to the left wing when she is pulled up short by Rupali's voice.)* I wanted to make a go of it, Mother. I was going to break the stereotype and prove to the world that mothers and daughters-in-law can be friends, even confidantes. But I didn't stand a chance. You were the mother of five sons. There were rumours that your husband was merely the front man, but what did you care, each of your sons was better-looking than most mortals and extraordinarily gifted to boot. No wonder you were confused at times and thought you hadn't merely given birth to the five Pandavas but that the only suitable bride for them in the whole world was their mother.

You hated me even before I stepped into your house. Not that I blame you. Our two families were the stuff of TV soaps or a Henry James novella depending on your point of view. You were old world, aristocratic and down-at-heel. We were nouveau riche with money pouring out of our ears. Your businesses were failing, but you never forgave my father for proffering my hand and lots of liquidity. *(Laughs.)* How uncouth we were. We thought cinema, Indian commercial cinema at that, was real life. For one of the pre-wedding parties, Papa hired a nautch girl. She didn't exactly do a cabaret but she did a mujra and sang. You sat through it and bore it with wounded dignity and barely concealed revulsion.

We may both loathe the prospect but I'm proving to be the daughter you never had. I too now tend to forget that all old money was nouveau riche at one time. *(She looks bewildered and tormented.)* Oh Ma, what makes us enemies? Is it something in the genes? Will I too hate my daughters-in-law? Sometimes I think the only thing experience teaches us is to make the same mistakes again. We talk of men as the villains but women are no better. It's not Indian husbands who burn their wives when they don't bring enough dowries. Mothers-in-law and sons do.

> *(Bimal enters with a clay pot in his hands and looks despairingly at both the women. He is a strong, powerful man.)*

BIMAL

Fifteen minutes, twenty on the outside, that is all the time it took for his shrunken, emaciated body to burn to ashes. *(He places the pot on a very low, broad, flat stool in a corner and puts flowers on the lid. He comes over and embraces his mother.)* Don't worry, Ma. Raj is no more but I'll take good care of you. I'll take charge of the business and make a multinational empire of it.

> *(Patting his cheek, Bimal's mother lets go of him. She looks at Rupali with intense loathing and exits. Bimal stands still for a few moments. He finds it difficult to contain his emotions.)*

I love you so much but I didn't want him to die. I really didn't. I know it sounds false but I loved him dearly.

RUPALI

I know you did; he was your brother. And so did I.

(She kisses him passionately.)

BIMAL

Am I happy? Or am I devastated? Since the day you were married I wanted him out of the way, but not like this.

RUPALI

Wishes don't kill people, Bimal. Besides, even when Raj was in the best of health, we were lovers regardless.

BIMAL

I never wanted you for a lover. *(Rupali looks puzzled.)* I wanted you all to myself.

RUPALI

But you already have a wife.

BIMAL

I don't care. I still don't want to share you with anyone.

RUPALI

(flares up) I'm sure she cares. And maybe you should find out if it's okay with me.

BIMAL

All right then, I will divorce her.

RUPALI

Just like that? Talaaq, talaaq, talaaq, three words and it's done?

BIMAL

(lost) Heads I lose, tails you win. You can't have it both ways.

RUPALI

Hush. Make love to me and wipe out the memory of how your brother suffered in the last few weeks.

(Fade out. When the lights come on, Rupali is fixing her sari and patting her hair in place.)

BIMAL
Will you marry me?

RUPALI
Isn't it a little premature? Your brother's ashes haven't even been immersed in the Ganga yet.

BIMAL
What is a decent interval?

RUPALI
Let's take it one day at a time, shall we?

BIMAL
(insistent) Say when.

RUPALI
Will you vote for me at the annual board meeting?

BIMAL
(flummoxed) Vote for you? What for?

RUPALI
As president and chairperson. Your five per cent stock will go a long way in getting me the job.

BIMAL
Is this some kind of joke? Or your notion of a trade-off? Our cousins, the consortium of our hundred dear cousins is baying at the doors with a deadly takeover bid, and you are playing the fool.

RUPALI
I'm in deadly earnest.

BIMAL
You? You are going to combat those vile and devious cousins of ours? You must be out of your mind. It's a man's game. I'll tell you

something else. Even Raj, your dead husband, couldn't have managed it. It's going to take all my resources to get the better of them.

RUPALI

You are right. They are vile, vicious and devious. And you, my friend, are going to be out of your depth. You think a little bit of blackmail, twisting of arms, greasing of palms, and if need be, a few hatchet jobs are going to do the trick. Wake up. We are talking arbitrage and leveraged buyouts here.

BIMAL

You think you are tougher? What do you know about business anyway?

RUPALI

Who do you think kept them at bay for two years? I held the fort, not your sick brother, and I didn't give an inch. They'll pull out every dirty trick in the book and then write a whole new one. But I'm my father's daughter. Shrewd, and if the occasion demands it, very, very devious and dangerous.

BIMAL

Our saviour and messiah, it turns out, is an Amazon, the new liberated woman. She'll outman any man and castrate him to prove the point. You did that to my poor brother but not to me, you won't. We were fourth-generation industrialists when your father set up his cycle repair shop. Go back to your papa, he'll buy you a toy company and underwrite your losses.

RUPALI

(truly hurt) Bimal, please. Please stop. We love each other too much to do this to each other. *(She takes a step and stretches out her hand to make up with him but he recoils.)*

BIMAL

Don't touch me. That lovey dovey act of yours won't work again.

RUPALI

(shaking her head) Is that what all these years together mean to you? Can't we keep the personal and the professional apart?

BIMAL

Do you take me for a fool? I know you are going to move in on my brothers and try to seduce them into voting for you. But even if you enlist one of them, it won't work. Ma hates you and won't ever let an outsider take control.

RUPALI

I'm as much family as you.

BIMAL

By marriage, not by blood and birth.

(Fade out. When the lights come on, Mother-in-law is cleaning uncooked rice in a stainless steel plate. Rupali is pacing back and forth.)

RUPALI

Seven live-in servants on call night and day but Mother has to make a show of how hard she works. *(She stops in front of her mother-in-law.)* Am I missing a subtle message here? That a woman's place is at home? I bring you good cheer, mother dear. Your son Bimal has had a change of heart. Starting with a passionate offer of marriage—no, he wouldn't hear of a decent interval after his brother's death—my erstwhile lover has now declared hostilities. In fact, I fear it's all-out war. And as a favour, a very special one, he let me in on a secret. He thinks you hate me, what an idea, and that you may not support my candidature for taking over our much-besieged industrial empire. *(There's a change in her mood.)* I didn't start it, Ma. I know you don't believe me but I loved Raj. He was unfaithful, whatever that wretched word means, for years, and I didn't know about it. When I learnt the truth, I wanted to sleep with the whole world. Anything to get back at him. I thought an affair with his brother would hurt him to the quick. I flaunted my liaisons. I thought he would get jealous and lock me up or tell me how I was sullying the family name. It didn't work. He was too busy either working or philandering at first and then with that terrible illness of his—I couldn't handle it. I had discovered promiscuity but I still wanted him back, chained and with a chastity belt.

Ah, the lady protests too much. I'm no nymphomaniac but I liked variety just as much as he did. I think we all do except most of us don't get a chance and so become self-righteous. Maybe that's what Draupadi's polyandry is about in the Mahabharata. About the compulsive human need for change and new experiences. Even her mother-in-law, Kunti, makes out with five males. The problem is banal but that doesn't make it any less real. We don't know how to square up this biological thing with our possessiveness and the mores of our society. That's the real dilemma of marriage, isn't it? Bimal and I and the rest of us are the same. We want free love for ourselves and monogamy and fidelity from our partners.

(Arun enters and hugs his mother.)

ARUN

Ma, I caught the earliest flight I could but I couldn't be with you when you needed me most. Isn't it strange, we all knew it was coming but that didn't prepare us for the real thing, did it? *(He looks at Rupali, disengages himself from his mother, walks over to Rupali. He holds her hands, then embraces her.)* What shall I say?

(Mother-in-law leaves.)

RUPALI

Don't. Just hold me and tell me everything will be all right. Tell me you missed me. Did you?

ARUN

Every minute. *(Smiles.)* No, that's an exaggeration. Every second minute.

RUPALI

That's neat. You were always good at credible lies. But you also missed your male friends just as much, didn't you?

ARUN

I am an artist, Rupali. Experience is the raw material of my art. More, more, more. The artist is insatiable.

RUPALI
You haven't told me a word about your trip.

ARUN
A triumph, nothing less. But for Raj's death, I would have been given a hero's welcome back.

RUPALI
(a little sardonically) You went, you saw, you conquered.

ARUN
That wouldn't be an exaggeration. The Lincoln Centre's invited me to choreograph a whole new ballet.

RUPALI
(genuinely pleased) Really? I am so proud of you. *(She embraces him.)* And what's it going to be about?

ARUN
The artist and society.

RUPALI
That will be your seventh ballet about the creative process.

ARUN
There's nothing in the world more mysterious and fascinating. What makes an artist tick? What is the source of his inspiration, his passions…

RUPALI
Oh God, how I miss my Raj. My poor, dear, honest Raj. Not a trace of chicanery about him, not even about his failings. Look at you and your fellow-artists. You think every journey you make is an odyssey but it always ends up at the same place. In front of the mirror, watching and cooing over yourselves.

ARUN
The artist is but a symbol of the conflict between the visionary and the conformist. Between the majority and the oppressed minorities. Like women, gays, untouchables, blacks.

RUPALI

Ah yes, all the right buzzwords. What if just this once you stopped making politically correct gestures and got your hands dirty with something that's real, something that twists your innards, something genuine for a change.

ARUN

How cruel you are. Do you know I live in dread of you?

RUPALI

Of me?

ARUN

When I come to you I'm reminded of those confidential charts in Raj's office. I'm consumed with fear and anxiety. Am I good enough in bed? Are the others better than I am? What if I can't make it? I keep feeling you maintain charts on all of us. And when we don't measure up, you drop us. I guess that's why I seek out men. I don't have to perform with them.

RUPALI

Isn't it tragic that we have converted sex into the last of the performing arts? Oh, let's not get depressed anymore. When do rehearsals start and when is the premiere?

ARUN

How will I go now that Raj's dead. All my life I've felt trapped. I wanted to be an artist, not a businessman. I want to be free, free, free.

RUPALI

I'll give you the freedom you so crave.

ARUN

And what happens to the business?

RUPALI

I'll take care of it. All you've got to do is vote me into the driver's seat at the board meeting.

ARUN
(doesn't like the sound of what he hears) You? What about Bimal?

RUPALI
Do you really think he's smart enough to fight off your predatory cousins?

ARUN
I have just five per cent stock.

RUPALI
That's ten between you and me. Your two younger brothers have five. If we can get them on our side, that's fifteen.

ARUN
(suddenly animated) Why didn't I think of that? We'll outmanoeuvre Bimal. I'll become chairman and president. With you as my assistant, we'll make a great team.

RUPALI
You can't be serious. Didn't you just say you hate business?

ARUN
This is different. This is a once-in-a-lifetime challenge.

RUPALI
Boy, are you slippery.

ARUN
(trapped and trying to cover up) I've a better idea. Why don't you become my personal advisor? Or a senior consultant to the company?

RUPALI
Let go, Arun. Stick to your role as choreographer and patron of the arts.

ARUN
I'll make a deal with you. I'll be chairman and make you president.

RUPALI

It won't work. Two people can't be in the driver's seat at the same time.

ARUN

I tried to do you a favour. I bent over backwards to accommodate you. But you can't bear the thought of sharing power with anyone.

RUPALI

(shakes her head) This is not one of your high-class PR assignments, Arun. It's a fight to the death with your cousins. You don't have the killer instinct.

ARUN

You are about to discover it. Bimal and I will gang up against you and throw you out.

(Fade out. When the lights come back, Mother-in-law is sitting centre stage. Rupali walks in.)

RUPALI

You win, Mother. Even Arun, for all his talk about how he wants to be an artist, won't back me. Do you know why? He too wants to be chairman. Happy?

MOTHER

(hands Rupali an envelope) That's my ten per cent and the five per cent of the youngest two. Signed and sealed. Neither Bimal nor Arun can stop you now.

(Fade out.)

CHORUS

I just made it to church that night of the Anne Frank play and went down on my knees. Don't snigger. Nazis too went to church and still do. I'm not sure whether ten years in prison is enough atonement for my Nazi sins. But since that day I have been looking for that common little face. Just let me get my hands on him. Do you want to know what that common little face looks like? Here. Take a mirror. *(Suddenly, floodlights are turned on the audience. The Chorus points to a man in the audience.)* That one. *(Four of the Angels run down in their hobnailed boots and drag the man up to the stage. The spotlight picks out the Chorus.)* When I act, I act swiftly. I don't waste time mincing words. No subtlety, no sophistication. Arse is arse for me, and spade is spade. Maid is maid and laid is laid. That's the way you like it, don't you? Fine. Then we won't wait for the court to sit. We'll start right now. Summary justice. Note the word summary. *(In an official voice, insert date and place according to the date and location of the performance.)* Date: Two thousand and dash-dash. Place: Dash-dash. Crime: On the day two tribals' eyes were gouged out and seventeen others burnt to death in their huts, you tut-tutted sorrowfully twice and slept soundly at night. Defendant: A common man. Sentence: *(Pauses)* The Price: Someone's got to pay the price for everything that happens in the world. Gouge out that bastard's eyes. *(About sixteen or twenty speakers have been fixed invisibly under the seats and on the auditorium walls. The spotlight picks out the member of the audience who is on the stage. Fingers approach his eyes. Then through the loudspeakers comes a bloodcurdling scream, cleaving through the sky and the earth and its very bowels. It fades as suddenly as it came on. The spot fades too.)*

ACT III, SCENE I

(The indicator reads: 'Hastinapur. The Palace of the Kauravas'. Dharmaraj knocks at the door. Sushyasan looks through the peephole.)

SUSHYASAN

(softly) Suyodhan, Suyodhan. We've trapped him. The lamb is ready for slaughter.

SUYODHAN

Send word to Uncle Shakuni. Ask him to set up the game.

SUSHYASAN

Shall I open the door?

SUYODHAN

What's the hurry?

(Dharmaraj knocks louder and more urgently. Stops, looks around and knocks again. After some time he gives up and turns away.)

SUYODHAN

(opening the door) Who's there? *(Dharmaraj turns around.)* Well, well, well, what a pleasant surprise. What brings you this way today?

DHARMARAJ

What brings me this way? Why, didn't you send me a most insistent invitation? Sushyasan has been coming over every day for the past month to remind me of it. 'Don't forget,' he said. 'We're playing dice on Thursday the 27th at ten in the morning. Suyodhan will be terribly disappointed if you don't come.'

SUYODHAN

Really? How strange. Come in, though. We might as well play a game or two now that you are here. Anyone there? Bring out the dice and counters.

(Servants come in with the paraphernalia of the dice game. Suyodhan and Dharmaraj sit down to play. Suyodhan rattles the dice in his cupped hands and then stops.)

SUYODHAN

What are the stakes going to be, Dharma?

DHARMARAJ

Our lives, of course. What else can Kshatriyas stake?

SUYODHAN

You have such a pretty turn of phrase, Dharma. *(Then a bit cutely.)* But it's only a game, isn't it, Dharmaraj?

DHARMARAJ

Of course, everything is a game: life, birth, death, caste, family, leisure, sex. It all depends on the way the dice fall.

SUYODHAN

Then one must choose one's dice carefully, mustn't one?

DHARMARAJ

I never bother to inspect my dice.

SUYODHAN

Maybe that's why you've never lost a game.

DHARMARAJ

It's not the dice, it's the player who matters. He must have faith in his own prowess. He must believe in himself.

SUYODHAN

Then there's no point playing. You win, Dharma, I don't have such profound faith in my abilities.

DHARMARAJ

Come, come. Didn't you say it's just a game?

SUYODHAN

Let's start, then.

(Dharmaraj throws the dice followed by Suyodhan. Suyodhan loses.)

DHARMARAJ

What will you contribute to my kitty, Suyodhan?

SUYODHAN

My string of pearls. Play, Dharma. Munimji, are you keeping the score? Play, Dharma. I owe you much that I must repay.

(Suyodhan is hounded by bad luck. The clerk barely gets a chance to lift his head.)

SUYODHAN

Damn my bastard luck. *(Each time the dice are thrown Suyodhan loses something of value. The names of blue-chip companies and other items that Suyodhan and Dharmaraj stake may be changed to make them relevant to the times and the country where the play is staged.)* The CIA files. The Peacock Throne. Our stud farm. NIA. Topkapi. All the rights to Deep Throat. Daughter of Deep Throat and Deeper than Deep Throat. The Andaman and Nicobar islands. The brothel chain from Santa Barbara to Bangkok. All our nuclear submarines. My collection of Chinese Ming jade. The Kohinoor diamond. Mitsubishi Corporation. The formula for the deadliest and latest in biological warfare. Our army. Our navy. Our air force.

SUSHYASAN

We're ruined. Stop it, Suyodhan. Shakuni-mama has let us down, the hoary bag of bones. Please stop before it's too late.

(Suyodhan shakes his head and continues playing.)

SUYODHAN

Interpol. All the rights to the numbers racket. The Brown Shirts.

SUSHYASAN

Where is that wretched uncle of ours? We are about to be pawned one by one and he sits in the toilet deep in transcendental meditation. Break down the door. Dynamite it and bring him out alive.

SUYODHAN

Chile. The Lockheed Corporation. All the rights to steel production up to 3000 AD.

(Shakuni-mama is dragged out, hastily doing up his dhoti.)

SUYODHAN

All the subjects of my kingdom.

SHAKUNI

You interrupted me.

SUSHYASAN

Uncle, has it got through to you that Suyodhan has already lost all our subjects? Now only we Kauravas are left.

SHAKUNI

So? What's the hurry? It'll take another seven days to lose the hundred Kauravas one at a time.

SUSHYASAN

Uncle, even if one, just one of my brothers is lost in this game, I swear by our gods I'll finish you off.

SHAKUNI

All right. All right. Cool down. There's no call for oaths and stuff. The world isn't coming to an end. Suyodhan, old man, you've been losing with such commendable determination, have you bothered to check the dice? No? I thought not. You're grown men now, married and all, but just as dumb as ever.

SUYODHAN

Belt up, Uncle, and keep your nose out of this. I want to play.

SHAKUNI

I came only because your brother dragged me out, old chap. Personally, I wouldn't dream of interrupting your run of bad luck. Even so, to play against the Pandavas, particularly against the man who happens to be just about the finest player in the world and not even to check the dice … tch, tch, tch. *(He shakes his head with disappointment.)* I don't mean to imply that Pandu's sons are cheats; but they are shrewd, clever, capable. If a king begins to vomit without rhyme or reason, one would naturally suspect that he's being poisoned, wouldn't one? Similarly, if a man wins, and continues to win non-stop, one is bound to suspect some hanky-panky. Dharmaraj, I'm sure you won't mind if I examine the dice, will you? I've always believed that those who are pure of heart have nothing to fear. *(Shakuni inspects the dice very closely.)* Nothing wrong with them. No place for doubt whatsoever. Suyodhan, you've already lost your subjects. Don't stop now. Go ahead and get rid of your brothers, your uncle and your parents. That will put paid to the whole dynasty.

SUYODHAN

Don't talk nonsense, Uncle. This is just a game. We're playing for fun. Dharmaraj is my cousin and a very great king. Would any self-respecting king pride himself on having conquered the Kaurava kingdom and the Kauravas themselves in a game of dice? The eldest Pandava, particularly, is righteousness incarnate. Why are you trying to create bad blood between us, Uncle? Come, Dharma. Play.

(Dharmaraj plays. His luck has turned.)

(Suyodhan eagerly throws the dice. He and his brothers jump up, freeze, do a soundless, wordless dance. Dharmaraj stares, stunned. The clerk recites the list of lost stakes backwards, beginning with the people of the kingdom.)

SUYODHAN

Have we won back all we had lost, Munimji?

MUNIMJI
Yes.

SUYODHAN
Well, Dharmaraj. What is going to be your first gift to me?

(Suyodhan continues throwing the dice and every stake Dharmaraj puts up is lost.)

DHARMARAJ
The crown jewels.

SUYODHAN
And?

DHARMARAJ
The cocaine racket.

SUYODHAN
And?

DHARMARAJ
The World Bank.

SUYODHAN
And?

DHARMARAJ
The plutonium reserves of the Pandavas.

SUYODHAN
And?

DHARMARAJ
The Aswan Dam.

SUYODHAN
And?

DHARMARAJ
The Mafia.

SUYODHAN
And?

DHARMARAJ
Mossad.

SUYODHAN
And?

DHARMARAJ
The northeast.

SUYODHAN
And?

DHARMARAJ
The west.

SUYODHAN
And? And and and and and and?

(With every 'and' he slaps his thigh.)

DHARMARAJ
The capital of my kingdom, Indraprastha.

SUYODHAN
And?

DHARMARAJ
My subjects.

SUYODHAN
And?

DHARMARAJ
Oh Lord, can't we stop now, Suyodhan?

SUYODHAN
And?

DHARMARAJ

Please, Suyodhan, let's call it a day. We've played our fill. There's nothing as prodigal as success. You have played fantastically and won fantastically. Let's stop now. My back is breaking.

SUYODHAN

And?

DHARMARAJ

Don't carry things too far, Suyodhan. Isn't it enough that I acknowledge total defeat?

SUYODHAN

And?

DHARMARAJ

My youngest brothers. Nakul and Sahadev.

SUYODHAN

(elated) Sumukh, harness twelve horses to our chariot and speed through time and space and ether to Indraprastha and bring Nakul and Sahadev here. Tell them, Dharmaraj bids them so. *(Ingratiatingly.)* You do, don't you, Dharmaraj? And?

DHARMARAJ

Bheem.

(Nakul and Sahadev enter and touch Dharmaraj's feet.)

NAKUL

Dada, you left for Hastinapur seventeen days ago saying you'd return soon. And that's the last we saw of you. No phone, no message, not a word. Everybody at home is sick with worry. What have you been doing?

(Dharmaraj does not answer.)

SUYODHAN

(emphasizing every syllable separately) Your Dada has been playing WITH—YOUR—LIVES.

SAHADEV

Dada, why is Suyodhan laughing so cruelly?

SUYODHAN

Dada, may we eat? Dada, may we fart? Full-grown men but can't do a bloody thing without Dada. You'll have to forget all your Dada-ing now. You are our servants. Sumukh, take that souped-up Rolls and go and get Bheem from Indraprastha. Step on the gas. Not a jot below 400 mph understand? Tell him, Dharmaraj bids him so. You do, don't you, Dharmaraj?

(Bheem enters and touches Dharmaraj's feet.)

KAURAVAS

Welcome, welcome. Wash your feet please. Done? Hang your shawl on the peg. Done? Come and sit down. Done? Now see what's in store for you. So? Don't you like what you see? You'll have to lump it then, won't you?

BHEEM

How are you, Dada? Have these people been treating you badly?

DHARMARAJ

No, not at all.

SUYODHAN

How else is one supposed to treat slaves?

BHEEM

(puzzled) Who's a slave?

SUYODHAN

You, Bheemrao. You are our slave. *(Bheem jumps at his throat and almost strangles him.)* What's happened to your tongue, Dharmaraj? Why don't you hammer some home truths into your brother's thick skull?

DHARMARAJ

Bheem, Bheem, let go of him. What he says is true.

(Bheem pushes Suyodhan away.)

BHEEM

What do you mean Dada, am I Suyodhan's slave? The Kauravas'slave? *(He suddenly notices the dice.)* Have you been playing dice, Dada? Who is left?

DHARMARAJ

Arjun, Draupadi and I.

BHEEM

(Bheem throws his arms around Dharmaraj.) Praise be the Lord. What more do we want? As long as you three are free, everything's fine.

SUYODHAN

Bravo! Kya deadly dialogue mara. Bheem, old man, you really astound me.

BHEEM

Dada, do me just this one favour. Forget everything that's happened, just get up and leave. We can't afford to lose anything more.

DHARMARAJ

Do you think I could leave you here like goods in a pawnshop and return home happy?

BHEEM

With you and Arjun safe, you can win back anything under the sun. Even Nakul, Sahadev and me.

DHARMARAJ

Don't worry. I'm going to win you back right now. Play Suyodhan.

(Suyodhan throws the dice before Bheem can stop him.)

SUYODHAN

And?

DHARMARAJ

Oh God, what have I done?

SUYODHAN

And?

DHARMARAJ
Arjun.

BHEEM
Please stop this, Dada.

SUYODHAN
Sumukh, take Father's Boeing 747 and bring Arjun here. Tell him, Dharmaraj bids him so. You do, don't you, Dharmaraj?

(Sumukh returns with Arjun.)

BHEEM
Arjun, you've got to tell him. Tell him.

(Bheem clings to Arjun's arms, weeping.)

ARJUN
Bheem. *(Raises him.)* Bheem, tears in your eyes? What am I supposed to tell, and to whom, Dharmaraj?

BHEEM
(laughs) What's the point of asking him? He's the one who needs sense put into his head. Dada has lost everything in a game of dice. We have nothing left. You are the latest victim. That leaves only Draupadi and Dada.

SUYODHAN
Well, Dharmaraj, shall I play?

ARJUN
I beg you, Dada. Stop the game. This has gone far enough.

DHARMARAJ
You are wasting your breath, Arjun. I'm not going to lose now. It's Suyodhan's turn to lose. I'm going to win. Win back each one of my brothers and every bit of our property.

ARJUN
Did a still, small voice from the heavens whisper that in your ear? *(Turns to Suyodhan.)* This game is over. Do you hear? Over.

DHARMARAJ

Don't you dare stop me now, Arjun. This is not the age of divine voices. I've consulted the Rand Corporation. Rand. Nothing can stop me from winning, they said. Computerized statistics. There's no way I can lose after losing so much. Play, Suyodhan.

(Suyodhan plays.)

SUYODHAN

(very softly) And?

KAURAVAS

(chanting the words in a rhythmic chorus like a mob at a football match) And and, and and, and and, and and…

DHARMARAJ

Draupadi.

SUYODHAN

Sushyasan, take my Concorde, crash through the sound barrier and bring our revered sister-in-law here. Tell her, her eldest husband bids her so. You do, don't you, Dharmaraj?

(Sushyasan exits and returns, dragging Draupadi after him.)

SUYODHAN

You will live to be a hundred years old, dear Bhabhiji. I was thinking this very moment that you ought to be here to witness your husband's victory, and there you are like some divine revelation.

DRAUPADI

Revelation? You mean a curse. The Kauravas play with me while my husbands watch the fun. Will you let go of my hand, Sushyasan, or do you want my nails to rip your face into shreds?

SUYODHAN

Sushyasan, let go of the lady's hand. She's delicate, though she has been handled rather a lot. You must remember she is our sister-in-law. Dharmaraj, are you going to play or are you going to save your own skin? The suspense is killing me.

DHARMARAJ
Play, Suyodhan.

ARJUN
Dada, please. Don't make this final mistake. If you don't rise to this bait, it will be Suyodhan's biggest defeat.

DHARMARAJ
The game's over. Suyodhan has thrown the dice.

(The Kauravas burst into hurrahs and yippees. Draupadi, who's been standing transfixed, now walks very slowly towards Dharmaraj. By the time she reaches him, the Kauravas' shouts have faded away. Everybody's attention is focussed on those two.)

DRAUPADI
What kind of game do you think you've been playing, my eldest husband and brother-in-law?

DHARMARAJ
The usual game, my dear. Dice. A miniature replica of life. Sometimes you win. Sometimes you lose. It was only a game, wasn't it, Suyodhan?

SUYODHAN
You mean something like house-house or doctor-doctor?

DHARMARAJ
Yes, wasn't it?

SUYODHAN
Sure, it was a game. Played in deadly earnest. You've merely lost your kingdom, your subjects, your estate, your brothers, yourself and Draupadi. For twelve full years you will go into exile. For one year after that you will live incognito. If anybody, slave or gentleman, recognizes you during that time, you will go back to another twelve years of exile.

DHARMARAJ
You can't be serious. When you were losing badly and about to stake

your brothers, didn't you assure Shakuni-mama that we were only playing for fun?

SUYODHAN

You aren't taking this in the right spirit, Dharmaraj. A man talks a lot of rubbish when he's losing. You're not supposed to take what he says seriously. Now that I've won, I mean every word I say. You watch. I'll sleep the peaceful sleep of the innocent from tonight, because now I really have a clean conscience.

DRAUPADI

So, Dharmaraj? All in fun, was it? You just decided to have a spot of fun gambling away your brothers and wife.

DHARMARAJ

Do you think I would have played with your lives if I had known that it wasn't a game?

DRAUPADI

If a man can play around with his loved ones in a game, can you imagine what he'd do with them in real life?

DHARMARAJ

That's unfair.

DRAUPADI

Nakul, Sahadev, Bheem, Arjun, me and then you. Tell me, how did you fix on this exact order of stakes?

DHARMARAJ

Simple. If I had staked myself first and lost, the game would have ended. And I'd have lost the chance to win back our kingdom and our subjects to which you and my brothers have as much right as I.

DRAUPADI

Played for kicks. *(She gives Dharmaraj a stinging slap across the face.)* Who do you think I am? A cow or buffalo or sheep from your farm or a multicoloured fish from your lake, or a chair, or your jester, or a rose or a peepul tree? Or do you think I'm the Nishat Garden from Kashmir or the nail of your little toe that you can so casually ruin my life when the mood takes you? And you, my gutless husbands? Where were you while your brother was busy distributing us around like largesse?

SAHADEV
Dada said everything would turn out all right.

DRAUPADI
He did, did he? And if he had told you to jump off the Eiffel Tower you would have done it, I suppose?

SAHADEV
Sure. Even if you'd told us.

(The Kauravas laugh. Draupadi hugs Nakul and Sahadev to her.)

DRAUPADI
God forbid that I should ever demand the most precious thing in your life. Your life itself. *(To Bheem.)* My fearless, full-blooded husband, there you stand, obsessively hugging your arms. And yet you couldn't use that magnificent body to save yourself, could you?

BHEEM
Draupadi, do you remember how I came by this amulet Dronacharya tied on my arm? I said I didn't believe in all this mumbo-jumbo. And do you know what he told me? 'This is not a lucky charm, Bheem. It won't change your future. It merely stands for a state of mind. It contains within it a commonplace but immortal platitude. Don't open it now.' He said, 'Some day, when you're wildly happy or sunk in despair, you will involuntarily hug your arms. Open the amulet then if you wish. Profundities are all right for philosophizing, but it is clichés that see us through life.' Today, when Dharmaraj lost, the amulet bit into my flesh. I opened it and found a note. It said, 'These days too will pass.' Draupadi, I promise you by everything I hold sacred, these days too will pass. Not of their own accord. But because I'll bring heaven and earth together to make them.

DRAUPADI

Our very lives have been destroyed and you sit there consoling yourself that these days too will pass? But tell me, Bheem, how did such days come to pass? Who cast this curse upon us?

BHEEM

I'm not praising myself, Draupadi, but honestly, after Dada staked me and lost the game, I pleaded with him to stop. What is the worst that Suyodhan and his ninety-nine brothers could have done to me? Worked me like a beast. It wouldn't have bothered me one bit. So long as I knew that you, Dada and Arjun were safe.

DRAUPADI

(moves back slowly, incredulously) God, how revolting you are. And how sick in the head. What has happened to that strong, upright body of yours, and that strong, straightforward mind inside it? All this pious rot about self-sacrifice and martyrdom. If this is how deep the canker has eaten, there's no hope for us. If a man will not fight for his own freedom, how can he be trusted with the freedom of others? *(Turning to Arjun.)* And you, I'm sure you too have a failsafe, foolproof alibi.

ARJUN

Let bygones be bygones, Draupadi. I begged Dada to stop playing. But what could he do? All the statistics were on his side. The Rand Corporation's report assured him of victory.

DRAUPADI

How could I have worshipped so callous and inhuman a man! Do you really believe that human beings are statistical figures to be quietly liquidated between the pages of a report?

DHARMARAJ

Draupadi, don't work yourself up like this. The fault is entirely mine. I see everything clearly now. The Kauravas played a crooked game. Any impartial inquiry would reveal Shakuni-mama's evil hand in all this.

DRAUPADI

Possibly. If you had won, people would have said the same thing about you. But that's beside the point. The only point is that nobody has a right over another's life. Enough talk. I'm off. I alone have the right over my life, and I'm going to use it to cut myself free from all of you.

SUYODHAN

Right? A slave has only one right. To obey his master's command. I've had my fill of your harangues. The sooner you accept your new status, the easier it'll be for you.

DRAUPADI

The new status is utterly irrelevant to me. I was once the wife of the Pandavas. But no longer. Goodbye.

SUSHYASAN

Not so fast. *(He pulls her by the end of her sari.)* Where do you think you are going, my lovely? *(She struggles.)* It won't take a jiffy to bring you down from your high horse. *(He fiddles with her blouse.)*

DRAUPADI

(kicks Sushyasan who is pawing her) Bheem, Arjun, save me. How can you let them do this to me? Oh God, Krishna, where are you?

SUSHYASAN

Didn't you just divorce them? Then why are you calling on them now? You've got all of us instead. *(He shows Draupadi his thigh.)* You'll never starve for sex again.

(Bheem lets out an enraged yell.)

BHEEM

Remember this, Sushyasan. One day I'll tear open that thigh and drink the blood from it or my name isn't Bheem.

DHARMARAJ

There's no point getting angry, Bheem. We can no longer afford that luxury.

DRAUPADI

Arjun, are you too going to listen to that jellyfish brother of yours? How can you bear to watch what's happening? Cleave Sushyasan with a single arrow and cover my nakedness in his blood.

ARJUN

How can I make you understand, Draupadi? We have lost. And under the law, losers have no rights.

DRAUPADI

Who has lost, Arjun? How can you submit to the outcome of a game that was played without your knowledge and without your consent?

ARJUN

It's a gentleman's agreement, Draupadi.

DRAUPADI

And you watch like a gentleman while the Kauravas manhandle me. *(She looks around at the gathering.)* Who do I see here today? The wisest and oldest upholders of our civilization. There they sit, the lecherous voyeurs, watching one of their senile fantasies come true. But mark my words, if you don't stop these blackguards now, the winds of war will sweep this land bare. Krishna, oh Lord Krishna, where are you?

KARNA

What sin is there in stripping the mistress of five men? Harlots don't cause wars nor does God appear at their bidding.

(Draupadi suddenly ceases to struggle. Sushyasan, nonplussed, stops his pawing. With half-undone blouse and trailing sari, Draupadi walks to Karna. As she approaches, Karna steps back uncertainly.)

DRAUPADI

Wait, Karna. *(She holds him by the arms and looks at him.)* Let me look at you. Let me look at the face of vengeance sated. Would you believe it if I told you that your joy today is the only thing I share with all my heart? I want to murder those old-maid husbands of mine, and those Kaurava barbarians, and all those dirty old men. Very slowly and painfully. But you? I can't forget the price you've had to pay for this moment. I want you to know that I will gladly give myself to you. Any time. Even if it is merely to satisfy a random lust.

SUSHYASAN

Draupadi, you can't leave the game halfway. We want a complete striptease. Start the music.

DRAUPADI

(screaming horribly when Sushyasan tries to pull off her sari) Stop this, Krishna, for God's sake, stop it. Lord, if only I could die. *(A sudden shaft of light reveals Krishna.)*

KRISHNA

Stop this demonic game. *(Places himself between Draupadi and the audience.)* No more of this perversion. I will not stand by and watch it.

DRAUPADI

Yet you watched long enough.

KRISHNA

I was waiting for your call.

DRAUPADI

What sort of God are you that needs calling?

KRISHNA

Do you think God is merely your local answering service? I'm here now, aren't I? That's what matters. Calm down, Draupadi. If I'd had a hint of this earlier, I would have stopped this whole shameful scheme of the Kauravas before it started.

DRAUPADI

Four years old when you opened your mouth to give Mother Yashoda a glimpse of the universe. And today a trivial matter like this didn't get through to your omniscience because some petty circuit or chip failed, I suppose.

KRISHNA

I was biding my time, Draupadi. I believe in giving people a long rope to hang themselves by.

DRAUPADI

And if an innocent woman gets caught up while you're busy doling out rope, so what?

KRISHNA

Didn't I come before anything untoward happened? Let anyone try to touch a hair of your head now.

DRAUPADI

No one here is interested in touching my hair.

KRISHNA

Stop playing with words, Draupadi.

DRAUPADI

Why? You didn't grow weary watching the Kauravas playing with me.

KRISHNA

How bitter you've grown in one day! How deeply these people must have hurt you. *(He takes her in his arms.)* My poor, tired, little child.

DRAUPADI

Krishna, take me home with you. *(Krishna starts and becomes wary.)* Please, I don't have an ounce of strength left in me now.

KRISHNA

Who am I to take you away, Draupadi? Your place is with your husbands.

DRAUPADI

But they've sold themselves, brains, souls, bodies and all. I'll have to go with you.

KRISHNA

That's not possible. You too have been exiled with them.

DRAUPADI

Aren't you God? My Vithoba, my Khandoba, my Pandurang, my Brahma? Then why do you continue to torment me? Just tell these people that nobody can stake me against my will.

KRISHNA

It's you who needs telling. I never meddle in the personal affairs of human beings. If I did, it would make nonsense of the doctrine of free will.

DRAUPADI

(she can't believe her ears) Free will? Then I'm telling you of my own free will to take me away from here. *(Krishna shakes his head.)* Then why have you come?

KRISHNA

To save you from the shameless Kauravas.

DRAUPADI

(goes over to the side of the Kauravas) How will a shameless God save me from shame? Nothing can shame me now. Instead of whoring for five men, I'll be mistress to a hundred. But never will I go back to the Pandavas or their God with a begging bowl.

ACT III, SCENE II

(The indicator reads: 'A hut in East Pakistan'. Seven soldiers kick open a door. A young mother is nursing her baby.)

FIRST SOLDIER
Where's Allauddin Mohammad?

SALMA
He's gone out. Only his mother, sister and I are here.

(She quickly draws her veil over her face. One of the soldiers rips it off.)

SECOND SOLDIER
What's happened to your veil may happen to other things if you don't talk straight. Where's that bastard Allauddin? We've heard he's become a major in the Mukti Bahini, after being a mere corporal in the Pakistani Army. Are you going to talk, or do you want your tongue ripped out?

SALMA
He's with his battalion.

FIRST SOLDIER
He is, is he? Well, we're in no hurry. While he's with his battalion, our battalion's with his wife. *(Suddenly pulls her hair.)* Talk. He's coming to see you tonight, isn't he? Out with it, you bitch.

SALMA
I have had neither message nor letter from him these five months.

FIRST SOLDIER
So that's your tune, is it? Well, see with your own eyes what we do to

that traitor husband of yours when he gets here. But we must prepare a treat for his eyes too, mustn't we? What're you waiting for, boys? Take the child. Boy or girl? Talk, you bitch, or we'll shoot its head off through the ceiling.

SALMA
Boy. His name is Salim.

FIRST SOLDIER
Fine, what difference does it make? Take the bastard.

SALMA
Don't, I beg you in the name of Allah. He's just a child.

SECOND SOLDIER
The children of traitors are traitors too.

SALMA
Please let my child go. He is not even a year old. I'll satisfy all of you.

FIRST SOLDIER
We don't need your permission for that. (*Dumps the child in its cradle.*) Get on with it, boys.

(Darkness. While the seventh soldier is still astride her, there's a shout offstage.)

FIRST SOLDIER
Allah. We're done for. The Indian Army and the Bahini. Run. Run for your lives. Run.

(All except the one still astride Salma run away. They return as Indian Army and Bahini men. They kick the door open. The man who is clinging to Salma is bayoneted by each one of them separately and then by all together. The woman shudders once, gripped by a spasm. Just once, soundlessly. Then they surround her.)

FIRST SOLDIER
Bitch. Slut. Even sluts are better. They at least do it for money. I tell you, men would be better off sleeping with dogs. Dogs don't betray

you. Poor Allauddin. He's risking his life for the freedom of millions of children and women like this one, and she's busy hoisting her petticoat every time she sees something dangling. God knows between whose legs my wife is finding happiness back home. What are you waiting for? Take her, the poor thing gets lonely without Allauddin.

(Darkness. The six men throw themselves on Salma one after the other. While the sixth is still on her, loud and impatient knocking is heard at the door.)

ALLAUDDIN

Salma, open the door, Salma. Mother, Dilwar, open the door. Don't be scared, Salma. It's me, Allauddin. Your husband.

(The sixth soldier buttons up his trousers and opens the door. Allauddin hesitates a moment, bewildered. A flicker of suspicion flashes across his face like a streak of lightning and then fades.)

ALLAUDDIN

Salam alequm my friends, my brothers. *(He embraces all the soldiers in turn. Salma pulls her veil over her face.)*

FIRST SOLDIER

We weren't sure who was knocking. We thought the Pakis had got us. Then we heard your familiar, impatient voice and we breathed freely again.

SECOND SOLDIER

(kicking the soldier they have killed) What a lucky coincidence that we were passing this way just when this bloody Pakistani soldier was entering your house. We finished him on the spot. What's new? Have they captured all the Pakistani troops stationed around here or have some escaped?

ALLAUDDIN

By the grace of Allah there's not a single Pakistani soldier left in this sector at least. By Monday, or at the latest, by Saturday, there'll be no East Pakistan left. It'll be Bangladesh.

FIRST SOLDIER

Then we will publicly parade, lynch and tar every Paki who brought suffering to our brothers and sisters.

ALLAUDDIN

May your words come true. Salma, I hope you have looked after our visitors. They are as brave as lions and loyal friends. We would give our lives for each other.

SALMA

I have looked after them as well as you could have wished.

SECOND SOLDIER

Bhabhiji's hospitality leaves nothing to be desired. We must go now. Major Ashraf must be wondering where we've vanished. See you soon.

ALLAUDDIN

Yes. See you in Bangladesh. *(They leave.)* Where's Mother? And Dilwar?

SALMA

(her voice comes greyly, as if through ashes) At the well. They left long ago. They'll be back soon.

ALLAUDDIN

I hope they take their time. I never get you to myself. How long is it since I saw you? Allah, how I used to ache with longing for you each night. How is he, our Salim? I see he's sleeping. Does he walk? Talk? Does he look like me? Why are you so quiet, Salma? Has something happened? *(He advances towards her. She starts and shrinks away. He laughs and keeps coming.)* Still as shy as you were two-and-a-half years ago on our wedding night. You're afraid, aren't you, that Dilwar and Mother might suddenly come and catch us in each other's arms? I don't care if they do. I want you now and nothing's going to stop me, not Mother, not Dilwar, not the entire Pakistani army.

(He embraces her. She picks up the bayonet and plunges it into him. He stumbles backwards and falls. She stands shivering slightly; then sits down, and quietly stabs him again and again twelve times. Fade out.

Floodlights pick out a woman at one of the auditorium exits. The Chorus enters. He begins to address her in the manner of an adult coaxing a child.)

CHORUS

Poor little thing, she's feeling sick. Did you do wee-wee in your panties when you heard those screams? Oh dear, dear, you fainted, eh? How nasty all this is. You wanted to slip off home on the quiet, did you? Got as far as the door. But the Chorus wasn't looking the other way and cleaning his ears. You've paid good money to see this play. How could I possibly let you go without giving you your money's worth of entertainment? *(Two of the Angels escort the woman to the stage.)* Don't feel shy, lady. You're quite strong on women's lib, aren't you? You don't approve of discrimination between men and women. Well, you can trust me not to show it. Stripping that poor woman, Draupadi, wasn't a nice thing to do, was it? Men are like that. Lowdown curs. But you too were there. Why didn't you crack Sushyasan's head open with an axe? Why didn't you scream the theatre down when these hirelings beat up one of you right here a while ago? But you didn't raise a whimper of protest. Had you lost your voice? No? Never mind. What's the use of keeping a tongue in your head if it doesn't do its work when required? Evolution took man's tail from him. One day it'll take away his tongue. The price. It's the same problem once more. Someone's got to pay the price for everything that happens in the world. *(The spotlight rests momentarily on the woman. A blade gleams in the light. One of the Angels forces her mouth open and pulls her tongue out.)* Chop off her tongue.

(A faint whimper as the lights go out.)

ACT IV, SCENE I

(The indicator reads: 'Hastinapur. The Durbar'. Suyodhan and his brothers are in the Hall of Audience. The Pandavas and Draupadi enter.)

SUYODHAN

Welcome, welcome. We've been waiting for you. This is indeed a great day. Brother meets brother after thirteen years. The Kauravas stand ready to greet their sister-in-law. Please sit down. We may be kings but we are your cousins first. There is no need to stand before us. Oh dear. Are there no chairs? They've all been sent off to Shivaji Park for tomorrow's mammoth meeting, I suppose. Never mind. No formalities. We shan't take offence if you continue standing.

DHARMARAJ

Suyodhan, in accordance with the promise we gave you, we remained in exile for twelve years. For one year after that we lived incognito. Nobody recognized us, so you cannot clamp another exile on us. We are confident that you and your brothers will now keep your end of the deal.

SUSHYASAN

Suyodhan, don't they look as if exile suits them? Look at that fabulous tan Draupadi's got. As for dancer-boy, he's looking as fresh as a blooming flower. His nose looks even more delicate and aquiline than it used to. And Superman's acquired such immense muscles that you can't take them all in at one glance. I don't think we have any right to take their exile away from them. As of today, let's bestow upon them unlimited exile.

ARJUN

Our debt of honour has been paid, Suyodhan. Return Indraprastha to us now.

SUYODHAN

Indraprastha? *(pauses)* Oh yes, Indraprastha ...your one-time capital. It suffered terribly after you went away. It became a desert, a vast wasteland, a graveyard broiled in the merciless sun. Finally we got fed up and literally gifted the place away to the Jews. They'd been after everybody's blood anyway about wanting a homeland of their own. We thought it would serve them right if we gave them Indraprastha. But those Jews, they'll make lotuses bloom in gutters and turn a desert into the Garden of Eden. That's just what they've done. Through nothing but sheer hard work. And brains. The place is unrecognizable now.

DHARMARAJ

We want Indraprastha. You and your brothers had pledged to return it.

SUYODHAN

Pledged? Like a lover to a beloved? How romantic and childlike you still are. The political scene is no longer what it used to be, you know. It's a whole new world now.

ARJUN

The Kauravas pledged themselves in the UN with several countries as witnesses.

SUYODHAN

Cut out that highfalutin nonsense about pledges and principles. When Mussolini invaded Abyssinia in the thirties, you Pandavas didn't lift a finger to give Haile Selassie the protection you had promised.

DHARMARAJ

Think again, Suyodhan. The house of the Pandavas has ruled over Indraprastha for two thousand years. And now, unwarned by precedent and uninfluenced by example, the Kauravas have broken their pledge. You are asking for war, and on my word, you shall have it with a vengeance.

SUYODHAN

Dharmaraj, we are meeting today after many years. There is so much to tell and so much to ask. We are consumed with curiosity about your innumerable new experiences. But it isn't possible today. Tensions and conflicts among nations have reached such proportions that we Kauravas finally decided to act promptly and decisively. Present in Hastinapur at the moment are the representatives of all the countries of the world. Today, the Kauravas will inaugurate the International Conference for Permanent Peace. We are certain that we carry your good wishes with us on this auspicious occasion. *(He is about to leave, but stops.)* Just one more thing. We have nothing to do with Indraprastha now, you know. Whatever your demands are, wouldn't it be more realistic for you to negotiate directly with the Jews themselves? *(Again he is about to leave.)*

ARJUN

(very controlled, but with cold hatred) Suyodhan. *(Suyodhan stops.)* War. Total war.

SUYODHAN

(throws his hands up) What can I say, it's the will of God.

ACT IV, SCENE II

(The indicator reads: 'The battlefield of Kurukshetra'. The screen at the back is lit up by small campfires. Every now and again squat, elongated or excessively broad shadows of people fall across it. A strong resonant voice bursts into song, which is heard sporadically. From somewhere come the sounds of a bhangda dance. Then all is strangely silent.)

ARJUN
(bitterly) It's almost like a picnic, isn't it?

KRISHNA
It is. One long, endless picnic.

ARJUN
Where's the bhangda going on? In Suyodhan's tent? Can't make out the tent flags in the dark.

KRISHNA
You're night blind. The bhangda's on at Ashwathama's. Suyodhan's got Mallika Pukhraj Begum singing at his place. Don't you remember? We were all invited. But you said you wanted to prepare for tomorrow.

ARJUN
Krishna, do you think her music will come out of tomorrow's holocaust unscathed?

KRISHNA
Why not? She's going to die someday, but it's not the war that's going to kill her. And anyway, there will always be her daughter to carry on the music.

ARJUN

You've neatly sidestepped my point, haven't you? Krishna, I fear that tomorrow's massacre is going to claim much more than just human life. It might permanently destroy a vital gene of humanity and we might start giving birth to monstrous, demonic children. Wittingly or unwittingly, our ancestors cultivated and nurtured this heritage of ours. They have passed it down to us with care and caution, sometimes stumbling, sometimes making terrible mistakes, but always trying to save it for us, a little at a time. And tomorrow we will let loose a tidal wave of deliberate destruction upon it all.

KRISHNA

A moving speech. And hopelessly shallow. Stop being sentimental, Arjun. I've always thought that sensitive people are a bit obscene. I feel nothing but contempt for the confusion in their thinking. You are fighting the war precisely to guard the heritage and values that are so dear to you. I hope you won't need to be reminded of this again. And now let's stop this lofty nonsense.

ARJUN

The same argument was used to justify the first and second World Wars.

KRISHNA

That doesn't make it less valid.

(Strains of 'Abhi to Main Jawan Hoon' are heard from Suyodhan's tent. Both listen in silence.)

KRISHNA

If you hadn't been pig-headed, we would have been listening to that superb singing.

ARJUN

You can see in the dark, can't you, Krishna? Whose tent stands next to Suyodhan's?

KRISHNA
Bheeshma's.

ARJUN
Next to his?

KRISHNA
Drona's.

ARJUN
And next to his?

KRISHNA
Sushyasan's.

ARJUN
And then?

KRISHNA
Karna's. And next to his is Shakuni-mama's. But foul play won't work now. Dronacharya has as many spies in our army as we have in theirs. Besides, even if you manage to bump off five or ten of the Kauravas, it will hardly make a dent.

ARJUN
How strangely you speak. The thought of foul play never crossed my mind. *(Pauses)* Krishna, this war is not going to be fought. Or if it is, it will be fought over my dead body. I will not spill the blood of my kinsmen.

KRISHNA
You are exhausted. Go and rest a while. The fate of the war will be decided tomorrow. But defeat or victory will depend entirely on your state of mind tonight. Beware the long and treacherous night, Arjun.

ARJUN
Do you know who taught me to fix an arrow to a bow? Dronacharya. Do you know who sent Dharmaraj and me to MIT? Bheeshma. Do you know who took me secretly to a doctor when I got gonorrhoea?

Suyodhan. I owe something to each one of the men in that camp, and each one of them owes something to my brothers and me. There's no greater bond than the daily give and take of life. The Kauravas are incomplete without the Pandavas, Krishna, and the Pandavas are the lesser without the Kauravas. We complement each other because we are each other, in turn and simultaneously. Apocalypse and annihilation sound like words out of the scriptures. But nuclear warfare and the climate crisis have made them as real to us as the earth we stand upon. What do you think will be left after this war, Krishna? Neither maya nor nothingness. And even if the Pandavas survive, who will they fight? Who will they love?

KRISHNA

I'm glad you've brought in big names like Bheeshma and Drona. Where was the honour of these honourable men when Draupadi's modesty was publicly outraged? The Kauravas are the cause of this Armageddon. They were the first to raise a hand. Anything the Paṇdavas do now is justified.

ARJUN

(thoroughly shaken, he speaks very slowly, but undramatically) Oh God! And to think that you are the First Cause. Aren't you the reason for all that happens on the earth?

KRISHNA

Touché. But this is not a game of rhetoric. I descend on earth when the sins of men multiply and cannot be contained. When a great leader is born into the world, it is his objectives, insight and vision that mark him from other men. The ordinary man may not understand the quality and depth of his vision, but he is willing to lay down his life for a Napoleon, Lincoln, Gandhi or Lenin. The leader, in his turn, then forgets his personal identity and takes upon himself a stupendous responsibility. Leadership is your dharma, your duty, Arjun. You cannot reject it. Most important of all, you must follow the dictates of your dharma without hope of reward, or fear of consequence. To think of consequences once a job is begun only serves to paralyse a man. Get up.

ARJUN

If one is not to take into account the fruits of one's actions, how does it matter whether the Pandavas or the Kauravas win? If every man must act in accordance with his dharma, or the role that is thrust upon him by life, it is Suyodhan's dharma to annihilate the Pandavas by any means, fair or foul. What then is the difference between right and wrong?

KRISHNA

Just this. Survival. It is the only truth. The rest is irrelevant. Remember what Anouilh's Becket tells Henry, 'We must only do, absurdly, what has been given to us to do, right to the end.' That's it. That's what the Bhagavad Gita is all about.

ARJUN

But that's not true, Krishna, tell me just once that that is not so. Tell me even if it leads to our annihilation, that we don't need to, that we don't have to keep on doing what has been given to us to do. That we can choose to do the contrary.

KRISHNA

Someday, sooner or later, you will grow up and realize there is no escape from your dharma.

ACT IV, SCENE III

(The indicator reads: 'Kurukshetra'. The noise of battle. Suddenly, Dronacharya and Arjun come face to face. The raised sword freezes in Arjun's hand. Dronacharya also stops. Arjun touches Dronacharya's feet and passes his hand over his own head.)

DRONA

May success bless your efforts. May you live long, Arjun. Arise. How are things going with you?

ARJUN

They are going, but I doubt if I'm responsible for them.

DRONA

This is hardly the time to talk in riddles.

ARJUN

Then tell me how you, my Drona, my Dronacharya, my guru, have come to be part of this war? How can you be the commander-in-chief of the enemy in this holocaust? Wasn't it you who taught me the difference between right and wrong, between the sighted and the blind?

DRONA

I taught you the principles of aerodynamics.

ARJUN

You taught me the oath of Hippocrates. You taught me that there's nothing more precious than life.

DRONA

I put you on your guard when you accidentally came by the formula for the fission bomb.

ARJUN

The Kauravas planned this war to destroy the Pandavas. Instead of halting this fratricide, you gave it the stamp and support of your leadership.

DRONA

I only expounded the possibilities of biological warfare.

ARJUN

Don't quibble, Dronacharya. One word from you would extinguish the flames that have turned Kurukshetra into an inferno.

DRONA

Needless to say, I shall not speak that word.

ARJUN

Do you care so deeply for the enemies of the Pandavas?

DRONA

Why should that surprise you? If I had been in the service of the Pandavas instead of the Kauravas, I would have done my duty towards you with just as much steadfastness and loyalty. I don't involve myself in questions of right and wrong. Values and ethics do not fall within my ambit. This is the age of specialization. Some people formulate policies. Others execute them. I am a technocrat. My sphere is marked by rigid limits. What matters to me, what gives me satisfaction, is to do my job well. God be with you. Farewell.

(As the lights dim, a song is heard in the background.)

Once the rockets are up,
Who cares where they come down.
That's not my department,
Says Werner Von Braun

ACT IV, SCENE IV

(The indicator reads: 'Kurukshetra. A Conference Room.')

KRISHNA

You have to just say the word and we can end the war today.

ARJUN

We have fought for five years, sixty more days won't make much of a difference. They will all have to surrender in two months. At the most, two-and-a-half.

KRISHNA

Time, time. Time slipping away continually, and with every second lost we lose hundreds of our youth. So many millions have been killed already.

ARJUN

How can I deny the truth of what you say, Krishna? But what answer do I give when the war is over and we stand facing the International War Crimes Tribunal? Do I tell them that I was the first man in the world to set the precedent for universal genocide by using the nuclear option? That I did it even though I was in full control of my faculties, mental and physical, and thus gave future generations the right to annihilate creation?

KRISHNA

You are a fool. War crimes tribunals are convened by the victors. The vanquished are always the criminals. The definition of victory is precisely this. The winner is always right. Now are you going to waste some more time playing around with words, or are you going to do something to save those millions of young men who are fighting for our country and our civilization? Arjun, there is no alternative to nuclear war. Get on with it and press that button.

ACT IV, SCENE V

(The indicator reads: 'Kurukshetra'. The deafening sounds of a series of explosions. They resound through the auditorium for almost ten seconds, then suddenly there is a profound silence. Arjun falls to his knees at the centre of the stage. He presses his hands hard against his ears and shakes his head like one demented.)

ARJUN

Stop, stop, stop. This silence will shatter my eardrums. *(Krishna enters, lifts Arjun gently by the hand, and points to the screen at the back. Far away there is a glow with tints of orange on the horizon.)*

KRISHNA

Look Arjun. Look. The sun is rising. *(Arjun looks. Half a minute's silence. Then a very faint but unmistakable expression of revulsion and despair crosses his face. He frees his hand from Krishna's grasp.)*

ARJUN

No, it is not. They are lighting the funeral pyres of the Kauravas.

(The chanting of 'Nainam Chhindanti Shastrani' from the Bhagvad Gita fills the air.)

ACT IV, SCENE VI

(The indicator reads: 'Kurukshetra'. The blindfolded Grandmother who has been telling her grandson stories comes centre stage as Gandhari. The screen at the back is suffused with red. The chanting of 'Nainam Chhindanti Shastrani' is gradually fading away.)

GANDHARI

Krishna, Krishna.

(Krishna comes to her.)

KRISHNA

What do you want, Gandhari?

GANDHARI

I want a shoulder, Krishna. I want to cry till my tears wash me away.

(Krishna is about to take Gandhari in his arms when she begins to remove the scarf from her eyes.)

KRISHNA

What are you doing, Gandhari? You have been true to your husband and your resolve for a hundred and fifty years. The first time you lifted your eyes to Dhritarashtra's blind face in the marriage hall, you stumbled in his darkness. For a moment the proud, radiant, vivacious Gandhari lost her equanimity because of the cruel game life had played with her. But only for a moment. Then you swallowed your bitter fury against this betrayal. You stepped open-eyed into your husband's blindness and became one with it. You became the ideal of womanhood. Every Hindu wife worships you and aspires to your self-sacrifice. The gods themselves stand in admiration and awe of you. Now in the twilight of your life, Gandhari, why do you suddenly want to look upon this frightening, pettifogging and ungrateful world?

GANDHARI

Fool. Fool. Fool that I am. Eternally foolish. Shamelessly foolish. If there's anything superhuman in my life it is this stubborn, barren foolishness of mine. If I am a symbol of womanhood, it's because I avenge myself on others by punishing myself. If no disaster befalls me, I create one myself. And then find profound satisfaction in that utterly feeble, self-deceptive sacrifice of mine. You called me radiant, proud, vivacious Gandhari. Take a good look at me. Pride and honour are not the small change of life that you can spend them indiscriminately, Krishna. Wasn't I cheated into marrying a blind man? Was that the end of the world? If the deception had really maddened me, I could have plunged my fingers into my father's eyes, hung my wedding ring in Dhritarashtra's nose, and walked out on him. Or I could have proudly and courageously accepted what had happened and ruled my kingdom with wide-open eyes. But then who would have given birth to this noble legend of the woman who chose darkness because her husband was blind? Every night for these hundred years when that blind man floundered in my bed, drops of black, poisonous hate and revulsion dripped into my closed eyes. But poison too can become an addiction, and if Dhritarashtra didn't come one night, my body would burn with longing.

I could have opened my eyes, Krishna, but I kept them shut. And yet, even as the bodies of the Kauravas burn upon the funeral pyres, you play cat and mouse with me. My blindness has cost me my hundred sons. How you've deceived us, Krishna. All, all of us. Foolish Suyodhan, my other foolish sons, my foolish husband, me and those poor, stupid Pandavas who are destined to inherit nothing but a blood-soaked wasteland.

But what's done is done. There's just one thing that remains, Krishna. Only one last act which will absolve me of all sins, and give meaning to my existence. It won't bring my dead sons back, but it will save all the generations to come. Krishna, I'm going to kill God. You. I will unbind my eyes at last and fix them on you. And turn you to ashes within a moment.

KRISHNA

Do it, Gandhari. Open those eyes of yours, more dazzling than a thousand suns, and burn me to ashes. You have spoken, Gandhari. You cannot go back on your word now. End my centuries of suffering once and for all. Don't make me wait any longer. Only you have the power to release me.

GANDHARI

Is this another con of yours? A slick trick to beguile me and make a fool of me? And, of course, to give fate the slip?

KRISHNA

How can I make you understand the loneliness of God, Gandhari? My shoulders are crushed by the weight of this world. What if I happen to be God? How much can I endure alone? Who can I turn to in my suffering? With every man that dies, a part of me dies. You are a mother. It is your privilege to weep over your dead sons. But how can you comprehend the extent of my loss? I was born with every Kaurava that was born, and died with every Kaurava who died. How many more years must I be tied to the grinding stone? How much longer must I work the wheel of life and death? Please, Gandhari. Release me once and for all.

GANDHARI

Hush, my God. Oh my beloved Krishna, you should not pay attention to the ranting of an old woman. Who but you can guide us? In whom can we put our faith if not in you? Whom will we worship? Who will explain to us the difference between right and wrong? Come, my Krishna. How tired you are. Come into my arms and sleep.

(The stage becomes dark. Krishna and Gandhari are replaced by the Chorus. He speaks for the first time with complete honesty.)

CHORUS

Oh God, I too had a dream. For a moment I thought Gandhari would succeed in freeing the whole human race from God. That no man would ever be caught in the clutches of God again. Foolish, foolish, foolish me. *(Pauses)* That's it. The play's over. The fake Mahabharata is done. What did Arjun say? 'I will not kill my brothers. God, this war will not be fought.' And you? Did one man or woman from amongst you stand up to support him in his great and inspiring rebellion? If I had heard even one, not more mind you, just one voice of protest, however feeble, however faint, my job here would have been accomplished. One green shoot of hope would have lived amongst these millions of corpses. Forget it. Why am I deluding myself? Let bygones be bygones.

But the price? You've also got this sentence by heart by now, haven't you? *(Smiles.)* Someone's got to pay the price for everything that happens in the world. You do agree, don't you, that someone must pay the price for this universal indifference, apathy and callousness? Fine. That's what I wanted to hear. Just as you pretend not to see what you do see, I too can pretend to hear what I don't really hear.

Now take off your clothes. There's no need to feel shame. After all, you've done without it for thousands of years when all kinds of terrible things were happening. So why pretend now? You might as well wash away this filthy, ugly, perverted play with a chemical bath. Okay. Open the gas chamber taps. Yes, you heard me right the first time. Open the gas chamber taps. God be with you. So long.

(The Chorus and the Angels put on their gas masks. White fumes begin to fill the auditorium.)

BACKGROUND NOTES

The Mahabharata is one of India's two most important epics. At its simplest, the Mahabharata is about the deadly enmity between two royal families, the Kauravas and the Pandavas, who are cousins. While the Pandavas are India's greatest warrior heroes and are even worshipped in parts of the country, Lord Krishna, the presiding deity of the Mahabharata, is India's most human and beloved of gods.

Each of the acts of *Bedtime Story* is based on a well-known episode from the Mahabharata. The episodes are summarized in the following pages.

Act I

Dronacharya was the revered guru of the five Pandava and the hundred Kaurava princes. He taught them the military arts. Ekalavya was a young tribal chieftain who came to Dronacharya for instruction in archery. Dronacharya refused to teach him the art since it was a privilege reserved for the higher castes alone. The youth made a clay image of Drona and practised before it as though Drona himself was present. Reports of his extraordinary skill reached Drona, who went to the forest to observe Ekalavya's prowess for himself. Ekalavya acknowledged Drona as his guru, whereupon Drona demanded the right thumb of the outcaste as gurudakshina, a gift or honorarium given to the teacher. Since implicit obedience on the part of the pupil was the cornerstone of the guru–shishya (teacher–student) relationship, Ekalavya immediately cut off his thumb, thus depriving himself of his facility in archery.

Act II

Draupadi was the daughter of the king of Panchal. Many princes sought her hand in marriage. So her father arranged a swayamwara, a marriage ceremony in which a girl chooses her husband from among several suitors. Often, a contest of skill was organized, and the bride 'chose' the victor as her husband.

At Draupadi's swayamwara, the contestants had to first lift a great bow fashioned specially for the occasion and then shoot an arrow through the eye of a fish overheard that revolved from a high pole – not looking at the target directly but at its reflection in a cauldron of oil.

Most of the suitors could not even lift the bow and none could hit the target. When Karna came forward, Draupadi haughtily refused him permission to compete as a suitor, as he was the son of a mere charioteer. Arjun eventually won the contest and was garlanded by an overjoyed Draupadi. As the Pandavas returned home with Arjun's bride, Arjun called out to his Mother, Kunti. 'A great gift have we obtained today.' Kunti unknowingly replied, 'Then share it with your brothers.' These fatal words, spoken by the mother, were as a law to the Pandavas. Draupadi was married to all five of them and it was arranged that she should stay for two days in the house of each brother in turn.

Karna was the illegitimate son of Kunti and Surya, the sun god, conceived before her marriage to Pandu. He was abandoned by his mother and brought up by a charioteer. Only Kunti and Lord Krishna were aware of his true parentage.

Act III

Duryodhan, the Kaurava prince, filled with envy at the growing power of the Pandavas, challenged the eldest Pandava brother, Dharmaraj, to a game of dice and asked his uncle Shakuni, an expert player, to play on his behalf. Shakuni used loaded dice and won every throw, and Dharmaraj lost all his possessions, his kingdom, his four brothers, himself, and finally Draupadi (in that order). Dushyasan was sent to fetch Draupadi to sweep the hall as a sign of servitude. She refused to come, saying that Dharmaraj had gambled himself away, and as a slave and not his own master, he had no right to stake her.

Dushyasan caught her by the hair and dragged her to the palace, where he attempted to tear off her clothes in front of the assembly. All this transpired in the presence of the Pandavas and though Draupadi entreated her husbands to intervene, they did not do anything as they were now slaves of the Kauravas. Her garments were, however, miraculously restored by Krishna to save her from shame.

As a result of the gambling match, the Pandavas were forced into exile for twelve years, plus one year when they had to live incognito. When they finally returned, the Kauravas refused to give them back their kingdom as promised.

N.B. The prefix 'Du' signifies bad or inauspicious in Sanskrit and was firmly attached to the names of the hundred Kauravas. On the contrary, the prefix 'Su' signifies good and auspicious. I thought it unlikely, to say the least, that a mother would choose the 'Du' suffix for her children.

Act IV

On the eve of the great battle between the Pandavas and Kauravas in Kurukshetra, Arjun saw in the ranks of the opposing army, a number of his own relatives and friends. He was horror-stricken at the thought of fighting against them and laid down his arms, saying he would rather be killed than kill. Lord Krishna, acting as his charioteer, took matters in hand and preached the doctrine of dharma to him. This is enshrined in the most famous of Hindu texts, the Bhagvad Gita. A man's soul, Krishna says, is immortal and independent of the body. It neither kills nor is killed and has no part in the actions of the body. He advises Arjun to perform the duties enjoined by his warrior caste. As a Kshatriya or warrior he must fight, but he must do so in a spirit of disinterestedness, without hope of reward or fear of consequence.

Gandhari was the wife of King Dhritarashtra and mother of the Kauravas. Because her husband was blind, Gandhari always wore a scarf over her eyes in solidarity.

First published in India in 2015 by Fourth Estate
An imprint of HarperCollins *Publishers*

Building 10, Tower A, 4th Floor, DLF Cyber City, Phase II,

Gurugram Haryana – 122002, India
www.harpercollins.co.in

P-ISBN: 978-93-5136-999-8
E-ISBN: 978-93-5177-000-8

2 4 6 8 10 9 7 5 3 1

Typeset in 11/14 Adobe Garamond Pro at
SURYA

Printed and bound at
MicroPrints India, New Delhi

Black Tulip

A Screenplay

Kiran Nagarkar

FOURTH ESTATE • *New Delhi*

CAST OF MAJOR CHARACTERS

Rani Agarkar: Yoga teacher
Regina Fielding: Additional Commissioner of Police (ACP)
Anzar Akhtar: Computer whiz

The Police

Mr Goray: Director General of Police (DGP)
Lily Pinto: Sub-Inspector, Bombay Police
Bilquis Khan: Deputy Commissioner of Police (DCP)
Karan Sharma: Deputy Commissioner of Police

Others

Firodia: Businessman, owner of an IT company
Abdulbhai: Rani's clearing agent
Noor Jehan: Abdulbhai's daughter
Mr and Mrs Nanda: Rani's yoga pupils
Manohar Sane: Minister for Home Affairs, Maharashtra
Saleh: Mafia don
Bijlee: Dancing girl from Rubaiyat Bar
Azeeza: Saleh's daughter

SCENE 1: CREDITS

Int. Day. A large empty room with a wooden floor.

This scene is shot in colour but with a black-and-white look. A grey wall with a tinge of chill blue. From the bottom of the screen a beautifully formed, shapely creature rises mysteriously, followed by its twin—a leg goes up, unhurriedly followed by the other. And then a slim, svelte living thing shoots up. Slowly it becomes clear this is a woman in a black leotard. The effect is chillingly cold, slightly distancing and utterly silent. A young woman who obviously knows her yoga is doing some of the most difficult and yet beautiful asanas. It's evident that she has the grace of a Nadia Comaneci. She performs the asanas slowly with a liquid movement that seems to be seamless as she moves from one asana to another. Halfway through, the titles come on unobtrusively on one or either side of the woman or, if she's doing a shirsasan, above her feet also.

SCENE 2

Int. Night. Rani's drawing room.

Tight close-up of TV screen. A riot-stricken area of a city. There's a hostile Hindu mob in a low-cost housing area, including a slum surrounded by skyscrapers and several five- and six-storeyed middle-class buildings. Hundreds of people looking down from the buildings.

A MAN FROM THE MOB

(shouting)

Step aside.

The crowd parts. The man runs, leaps in the air and kicks a door. A mob of young men and women follow him. The door breaks open. Cut to the mob dragging out an elderly Muslim couple and a woman with two small children.

THE MOB

(chanting)

Kill. Kill. Kill.

ADDITIONAL COMMISSIONER OF POLICE REGINA FIELDING WITH A MEGAPHONE

Stop.There's been enough violence.

Regina Fielding walks towards the crowd. She's in her mid-thirties; she's a woman who downplays her good looks by seeming aloof. The crowd begins to close in on her.

MAN

If you know what's good for you, bitch, leave. Now.

Regina continues to walk through the crowd. A man lights the wick of a bottle filled with kerosene and hurls it at Regina. Regina catches it with her right hand. A young hooligan moves in on her with a long knife. Regina's eyes are devoid of all emotion as she watches the hooligan. Suddenly, she makes as if she's going to throw the Molotov cocktail at him. He flinches and ducks. Regina flings the lit bottle out into the empty playground beyond the slum where it bursts with a loud explosion. Regina keeps walking. The hoodlum slashes at her leather jacket with 'Police' written on the back and makes a diagonal cut across the leather and her shirt.

REGINA

You better kill me or give me the knife.

Tense silence. Regina takes the knife from the man and turns on her heels. Slowly the crowd parts. Regina takes the two children in her arms, kisses them on their cheeks. The children's mother and grandparents follow Regina. In the distance you hear a police siren.

Camera now pulls back from the tight close-up of the TV screen to show a woman practising sleight-of-hand magic tricks, which are a secondary leitmotif of the film. The tricks are intricate, complex and superbly executed.

RANI

(admiringly)

You better kill me … or give me the knife. Isn't she something else?

SCENE 3

Int. Day. Office of the Director General of Police

DGP GORAY

(talking on the phone)

How would you like to come back to Mumbai, Regina?

REGINA'S V.O.

Would you like a diplomatic answer or the truth, sir?

DGP GORAY

Let's try the truth.

REGINA'S V.O.

Too much politics and intrigue, sir.

DGP GORAY

That's why I need someone I can trust.

SCENE 4

Int. Early morning. Bedroom of a huge seafront apartment.

Rani, the yoga-teacher, is twenty-three years old. She's giving yoga lessons to Mr and Mrs Nanda. The Nandas are rich industrialists. The doors of the bedroom where the lesson is being conducted open out on to the terrace facing a tumultous, monsoon sea. The last part of that morning's session is under way.

RANI

(speaking slowly in a hypnotic but monotonous voice)

The perfect state of rest is death. The shavasan is a brief death. A time when your body and mind come to a standstill. We'll start with your right foot. Let life recede from it.

Camera cuts to the sea. When it returns to the bedroom, Rani is in the last stages of the yoga lesson. Mr and Mrs Nanda are lying flat on their backs with their feet spread slightly apart and eyes closed. They are in Issaye Miyake workout clothes.

RANI

Now that the eyes, nose and ears are dead, it's time to put the brain and the mind to sleep.

The Nandas are deep in shavasan and unaware of their surroundings. Rani wears thin surgical gloves as she walks towards a Burmese lacquer sewing box sitting on one of the shelves on the side, picks the lock with a paper clip and removes the keys from the bottom compartment. She unlocks the wardrobe door and gently opens it. She pulls back racks of clothes to reveal a big recessed safe. All the while, her toneless patter continues. She selects two keys and turns one anticlockwise and the other clockwise. Rani presses hard on the door of the safe and eases it out. There are twenty wads of brand new one-thousand-rupee notes which she puts in her extra-large leather shoulder bag. She picks up the full selection of exquisite ancient jewellery pieces which are obviously heirlooms, carefully makes room between the wads of notes. She places her scarf on top of the loot but leaves the bag open. She now slips in a printed note into the safe. It reads: 'You'll recover because you're insured. Black Tulip.' *Next to the last two words is the picture of a black tulip. Rani closes the safe door, locks it and closes the door of the wardrobe. She puts the keys back in the lacquer box and the box back in its place. Now she places the leather handbag on the floor next to the two inert figures.*

SCENE 5

Ext. Day. Street.

A street theatre performance. Rani is dressed as an impoverished farmer's wife and her friend, Lily Pinto plays her daughter. The farmer's wife addresses a minister dressed in the standard white clothes of a politician.

FARMER'S WIFE

My husband's been fasting for forty days to protest your indifference to the plight of the farmers, Minister. And now like my sons who are no more, he too is dying.

MINISTER

He would have died of starvation anyway if he had stayed in his village.

(farmer's daughter rushes in)

FARMER'S DAUGHTER

Ma, Father's breathed his last.

(mother and daughter break down)

FARMER'S WIFE

Now my husband's dead, how can my daughter and I cultivate our farm without water?

FARMER'S DAUGHTER

You and your cronies have swallowed all the money meant for irrigation schemes in the last eleven years.

MINISTER

What do you expect me to do if it doesn't rain? Collect the piss of all the Mumbai residents and fill your lakes?

(The audience boos and one of them throws a bottle at the minister)

GROUP CHORUS

This man is a mass murderer. Because of his greed and indifference, thousands of farmers are committing suicide.

Kaun Ram, kaun haram
Yeh aap theek jaante hain
Toh zubaan pe taala kyon?
Khula awaz oothao
Gunahgaron ko saza do.
Woh subah kabhi to ayegi
Woh subah kabhi to …

Audience claps. Lily Pinto approaches Rani and speaks softly to her.

LILY

I've to rush. My new boss, Additional Commissioner of Police Regina Fielding is taking charge from today.

SCENE 6

Int. Day. The International Library in Bandra-Kurla Complex

Rani is sitting at a table reading First Editions. She's trying hard to concentrate and take notes but there's a young man across with earphones, sitting at a computer and clicking occasionally while conducting the New York Philharmonic playing Beethoven's Ninth Symphony. Every now and then, sound leaks from his earphones.

ANZAR

Let's see what emails I've got today. Okay, download file. Wow, another piddling job.

RANI

(fiercely)

Exhibitionist. Pssssssst.

The man looks up at her, is oblivious of her angry expression, smiles charmingly and gets back to his computer, the symphony and the whispering. Rani gets up, yawns, looks around and walks towards some bookshelves. En route she glances at the young man's computer screen. He's obviously writing software. The young man's hand is asking the brass section to inject some life into their playing. Rani is busy pretending to look at some book while keeping an eye on the him. She notices that he has taken off his shoes. His T-shirt is clean but has holes in it. On her way back, Rani drops her book on the man's keyboard. His work is scrambled but Rani makes things deliberately worse by fumbling with the book. The man is furious and takes his earphones off.

RANI

I'm sorry. This floor is so slippery, I almost broke my neck.

(She deliberately continues to mess up his work.)

ANZAR

It's just six months of work gone down the tubes. I'm glad your neck is intact. *(Rani smiles sweetly.)* You're sure no bone in your body is broken?

RANI

I'm fine, thank you.

ANZAR

Your teeth, I hope one of them hasn't got chipped. Otherwise, like the Americans, you'll sue me for your fall.

RANI

I assure you all my thirty-two teeth are intact.

(As Rani moves away, she picks up one of the man's shoes and throws it in the litter can.)

ANZAR

(Speaks in a teary voice as he slaps the palm of his hand on his head. It should be clear that Rani can hear him.)

Damn. Six months of work.

SCENE 7

Int. Night. The International Library.

The bell rings and there's an announcement on the speakers.

V.O.

This is the last bell. It's five to seven. All lights will go off at seven. Please vacate the premises.

Anzar walks past Rani, looking worried.

RANI

What's the matter?

ANZAR

I seem to have left home with just one shoe. Maybe my mother's right. No one will marry me because I'm just a geek.

RANI

(exaggeratedly)

Oh no. Your mother's quite mistaken. You cut a fine, dashing figure. Even now.

ANZAR

Sure. I must be Valentino.

RANI

More like Tom Cruise. Just a haircut, a shampoo and shower, halfway decent clothes, a pair of shoes instead of just the one, a T-shirt with fewer holes, a belt that doesn't leave three loops out and maybe an all-new you, and you could look smashing.

V.O.

Everybody leave, please. We are about to close the doors of the library.

RANI

Is that your shoe there?

SCENE 8

Int. Early morning. The Nanda bedroom.

Mrs And Mr Nanda are dressed in workout clothes and sitting in the lotus pose but there is a feeling of unease.

RANI

Let's start.

(She enunciates the first word with which all yoga exercises start, with a perfect accent and the right weight.)

Om.

Before the two repeat the Om, Mr Nanda blurts out.

MR NANDA

The police want to see you about the theft.

Absolute silence. Tight close-up of Rani's face. It's expressionless.

MRS NANDA

Did you read in the papers that there was a robbery in our house?

Rani nods her head slowly. Mrs Nanda is close to tears.

MRS NANDA

Mr Nanda and I told the police that you were our dear friend and utterly trustworthy.

MR NANDA

But they said they had to talk to all those in the house and everybody who visited our house that day. The plumber, the security people, servants, milkman, neighbours.

MR NANDA

The family too. More than forty people.

MRS NANDA

We told them to leave you alone.

RANI

Hmmmm.

MR NANDA

(in his gruff, taciturn fashion)

Then you are not angry?

RANI

(shakes her head)

I'm mad as hell. *(Pause)* How are they going to find the robbers if you don't allow them to do their job? How much was that jewellery worth?

MRS NANDA

Seven crore. Maybe more. And there was some loose cash too.

RANI

When do they want to talk to me?

SCENE 9

Ext. Day. Outside Rani's apartment complex.

Rani exits the building with her fingers stuffed in her ears. The lane in which her building is located is always congested with cars honking non-

stop. There's a traffic jam right now. A policeman at the other end is trying to unravel the snarled traffic but the owners and drivers of Mercedes Benzes, Toyota SUVs, Porsches, Honda Civics, Ford Ikons, BMWs and others don't take their hands off their horns. Rani walks on the pavement and when she comes to a particularly obstreperous car-owner, she smiles sweetly, points to a sign that says 'SILENCE ZONE. HOSPITAL'. The car owner keeps honking and shows her two fingers. She continues to smile and walks to the next car with her index fingers again in her ears. Once again she points to the signboard. This time around the driver yells 'Fuck off' while hitting the horn even harder. Rani, still smiling, shrugs her shoulders and plugs her ears with her index fingers again. She is wearing capris and a T-shirt and is sporting a ponytail. She should come across as funny as she walks with her ears plugged. She turns into an apartment block, not her own, disappears behind a compound wall that is all brick and concrete up to a height of five feet and then has a latticed concrete grill. Rani opens her bag, takes out an Indian catapult, bends down, chooses two roundish stones, and places them on the brick and concrete wall. There are lots of shady trees in this lane and in the compound. She places a rounded stone in the back-end of the catapult, pulls the straps tight, aims and lets go. You hear the windshield of the car whose owner she had first addressed crack and the owner screaming and getting out of the car. Rani has already flung the other stone and hit the windshield of the second car. Chaos ensues. Now all the cars on the road are honking. Cut to Rani coming out of another gate. She continues to walk with her ears still plugged.

SCENE 10

Ext. Day. Outside Sterling Cinema.

Anzar walking out of Cyberia Café diagonally opposite Sterling Cinema. He's in his own world but as he walks past Sterling he sees Rani standing in a queue at the current booking counter for a thriller called If Looks Could Kill. *He looks at her, walks past her, comes back and stands in the queue behind her. Rani turns around. Anzar pretends to be engrossed in a technical book about software.*

RANI

Fancy meeting you here.

ANZAR

Why are you following me everywhere?

RANI

I'm ahead of you. So you must be stalking me.

ANZAR

(sniggers)

You wish. I watch every movie in town.

RANI

Go back to your book.

Cut to Rani in the theatre, all tensed up, watching as a man on the screen is about to stab the heroine while she's sleeping. A sound is heard at the crucial moment. Anzar, who has thrown his head back, is fast asleep and snoring steadily. Rani, who's sitting behind him, shoves his head forward. He gets up with a start, sits up, looks around and falls asleep again. Cut to Rani and Anzar coming out of the theatre along with the rest of the crowd.

ANZAR

Did you like it?

RANI

Great songs.

ANZAR

Absolutely superb. I loved the reggae numbers.

RANI

It was a thriller, stupid. There wasn't a single song or dance.
You snored right through it.

ANZAR

Nonsense. I never snore.

SCENE 11

Ext. Evening. Chowpatty.

An impromptu street theatre group is performing. A placard says The Houri Jannat Bar. Four girls including Rani and Lily dancing energetically to 'Kajra re...' *Suddenly, within the play, there's a police raid and the home minister enters.*

MINISTER

I will not allow these shameless women to practise their trade and ruin our menfolk. Lock the place up once and for all.

RANI

(speaking as a dancing girl)

But this is our livelihood.

MINISTER

Get a decent job as a secretary or receptionist.

SECOND DANCING GIRL

You need at least a BA degree for that. Most of us haven't even finished school. Besides, the Supreme Court has given a clear judgement in favour of dancing girls.

MINISTER

There's only one court as far as you are concerned. That's me. I will not permit you to desecrate our 3000-year-old Hindu culture.

The dancing girls sing

Kaun Ram, kaun haram
Yeh aap theek jaante hain
Toh zubaan pe taala kyon?
Khula awaz oothao
Gunahgaron ko saza do.
Woh subah kabhi to ayegi
Woh subah kabhi to ...

SCENE 12

Int. Evening. Rani's drawing room.

Extreme close-up of TV screen. Video footage of Grant Road Station. A man holds a gun to a woman's head. He's behind her and has his arm tightly wound around her neck. The woman screams.

MAN

Shut the fuck up. Shut up, shut up.

He looks across at ACP Regina who has him in the line of sight of her gun. Across from Regina on the other side is a colleague of hers, a male police officer. He too is pointing his gun at the criminal holding the woman hostage. A train rounds a corner and comes into the station. Man begins to drag the hostage towards a door of the train.

MAN

(shouting)

Drop your gun. You too. *(Pause)* I said drop your guns.

People pour out. Man fires a shot in the air.

MAN

(shouting)

Nobody move.

Everybody scatters. Man with the gun turns to the male police officer.

You want me to kill her? No problem.

Male police officer bends down and drops his gun. Man is next to train door now.

MAN

(yells)

You too.

Regina bends down and drops her gun. Then, suddenly, she looks in the direction opposite to the one where the man is holding the hostage. Her mouth has fallen open. Involuntarily, the man too follows Regina's gaze.

out of the house. *(Long silence.)* You are a hard-hearted woman. There's not a tear in your eyes.

RANI

You can't see it but my heart's bleeding. How do you manage?

ANZAR

Do the odd job, write some easy software. Mostly live off my mother's bounty.

RANI

Your father was right. You are never going to stand on your own feet.

ANZAR

(looks Rani in the eye but with barely suppressed anger and passion)

Do you know what I told him? You watch, Pop, I am not going to be bigger than you. I'm going to be bigger than Gates and Jobs put together.

RANI

(laughs)

Oh yeah?

ANZAR

Papa laughed too. But I will have the last laugh. *(Calms down.)* All I need is one of those superb new packages like Lightning III which speeds up calculations by ten to fifteen thousand times the current speed.

RANI

So?

ANZAR

They cost a bomb.

RANI

So you think once you have one of them, it will work wonders?

ANZAR

They're just tools. I'm the one who will work wonders. What about you?

RANI

What about me?

ANZAR

The deal was to exchange autobiographies.

RANI

Sorry, I've a six o'clock yoga session tomorrow with the Microsoft executives.

SCENE 15

Int. Evening. The International Library.

Anzar is engrossed in his work at the computer terminal. Rani stands behind the monitor and makes all kinds of faces and semaphore signals to get Anzar's attention but fails to do so. She turns around, picks up a sheet of paper, scribbles something on it with a marker, cuts off a bit of sticking tape lying on the next table and sticks the paper on top of the computer so that the paper covers the computer screen. The message on the paper reads: 'Closed for the night'. *Anzar reads the message, arches and raises his eyebrows rapidly as if to ask 'What's up?'*

RANI

I have a confession to make. The first time I saw you here, I was so pissed off with you for noisily conducting that virtual orchestra, I deliberately dropped the book on the keyboard and ruined six months of your work. I'm sorry.

ANZAR

I too have a confession. Even the most stupid computer nerd will back up every single thing he does at least twice, if not thrice over.

RANI

(does a double take at Anzar's confession)

You mean you were just guilt-tripping me with that sob story of yours?

ANZAR

Anything to catch your eye.

RANI

(in a dudgeon)

You will pay for this. Get up, we're leaving. You need fresh air.

ANZAR

(shakes his head sadly)

I'm allergic to it. Go into shock every time I breathe pure oxygen.

RANI

Let's go.

ANZAR

Where?

RANI

I'm taking you out tonight.

ANZAR

Go out with an unmarried woman? What will my mother say?

RANI

(makes a face as if to say, give me a break)

Pick me up at nine.

SCENE 16

Int. Late night. The revolving restaurant at the Ambassador.

RANI

I've got something for you.

ANZAR

One more T-shirt? Or a Fair & Lovely cream for the wheat-skinned?

RANI

Ingrate.

ANZAR

What have you got?

RANI

I'm going to make you crawl for it.

Anzar instantly goes on his knees and crawls all over the restaurant.

RANI

(whispers, embarrassed)

Get back, Anzar, stop it. Everybody's staring at us.

Anzar is busy picking up the ends of saris, lifting people's shoes. A worried steward rushes to Anzar.

STEWARD

Can I help you, sir?

ANZAR

(in a stage whisper)

My girlfriend's dropped my great grandmother's three-crore
diamond necklace and I can't find it.

Rani is now next to Anzar and on her knees.

RANI

This is the end, my friend. Finis. I'm through with you.

ANZAR

(whispers, choked with emotion)

If anyone finds the necklace, will you please hand it over to me?
I know three crore is not much but I don't know how
I'll face my grandmother.

Everybody in the restaurant is down on his or her knees, looking for the necklace now. Anzar and Rani get up, look at each other and make a quiet getaway. Cut to them outside the restaurant. Cut to them sitting on the parapet at Marine Drive. Rani takes out a small package from her leather handbag and puts it in the palm of his hand.

ANZAR

What's that?

RANI

A roach trap.

ANZAR

(Tears open the package. He can now see the print. Sheer wonder in his voice.)

Pluto 7. Where did you get it? That's ten times the speed of Lightning III. Besides, it's not even available here.

RANI

A yoga client collects software. If it's new, he's got to have it. Never mind if he doesn't even open the package.

ANZAR

This must be one hell of a rich dude. You know what Pluto 7 is going to sell at?

RANI

Hey, do you want it or not? I thought you said the only reason you hadn't made your first million was because you couldn't lay your hands on Lightning III.

ANZAR

(hugs Rani impulsively and withdraws quickly)

Thirty-three and one-third per cent of every dollar I earn is yours.

RANI

What does it take to talk? Make a legal contract and sign it.

ANZAR

You are going to be a very, very, very rich woman.

SCENE 17

Int. Night. Home Minister Manohar Sane's cabin in Mantralaya with his nameplate on the door.

Minister's secretary enters.

MINISTER SANE

No more calls till I tell you. And no visitors either. Now leave me alone. *(Keys in number and starts speaking on his cell phone.)* Don't worry about the new lady cop. I'm sure you can teach her a few lessons. Besides, she'll be transferred in no time.

SCENE 18

Int. Day. An interrogation cell.

Chhota Peg, a young man with flashy shiny clothes and a cocky attitude but not too much education, is sitting at a table. Interrogating him are two police officers, one a man and the other a woman. The woman, DCP Pande, is the retiring type while the man, DCP Karan Sharma, is relentless. Regina is watching from behind the one-way viewing window.

CHHOTA PEG

Sure, ask me anything you want.

DEPUTY COMMISIONER OF POLICE PANDE

You want us to believe you found Rs 14,000 on the road, Chhota Peg?

CHHOTA PEG

Finders takers.

DCP PANDE

I should hang out with you. Last time you were here you had come by Rs 17,000.

CHHOTA PEG

What can I say? I'm just a lucky guy.

DCP Sharma walks over to Chhota Peg, smiles at him and knocks his baton hard on Chhota Peg's shin. He jumps up in pain.

DCP SHARMA

You were right. Today's your lucky day.

DCP Sharma hits him again on the shin.

CHHOTA PEG

(in severe pain)

How come you always pick on the small fish and never the big ones? The guys who pocket 14,000 crore in one shot always go scot-free.

DCP PANDE

You give us the big fish and we'll let you go. We'll even say thank you.

CHHOTA PEG

You know the big names better than I do. Half the police department is in the pay of Salehbhai. Shantaram's hiding behind the defence minister's apron. Noorbhai is shacked up with that ex-actress in Bangalore. Get a warrant and get them. I'm just a pick-up and delivery boy.

DCP SHARMA

I bet even Salehbhai, the boss of bosses, would tell us he was merely a pick-up and delivery boy. What's the word on the street? Give us some hot tips. Our bosses are making life impossible for us.

CHHOTA PEG

(looking at DCP Sharma with contempt)

Any dance girl at the Rubaiyat Bar will know more than I do. Talk to Bijlee. She used to be Salahbhai's keep at one time. Even bore him a son. I'm not family. If I was, you wouldn't dare touch me.

The phone rings. DCP Sharma picks it up. Cut to Regina talking on the phone.

REGINA

Let him go. Just tell him to call or drop by if he hears of anything really big.

SCENE 19

Int. Evening. In an Udipi coffeehouse.

Rani and Sub-Inspector Lily Pinto in police uniform are having coffee in stainless steel glasses and a masala dosa. The policewoman is delighted to be sitting and chatting with Rani.

RANI

I want you to be the lead singer next time.

LILY

(blushing)

Me? I can't.

RANI

(smiling)

Of course you can. You must learn to project your voice, that's all.

(Rani smiles and pats Lily Pinto's hand.)

LILY

How could I ever say no to you? You stood like a wall between that awful director of the orphanage and me. She would cane you but you did not allow her to touch me.

RANI

(smiles)

We gave back as good as we got, remember? Hey, didn't you say you had a new boss?

LILY

I get to see her mostly on the parade grounds if I have morning duty.

RANI

Is she turning the police force upside down?

LILY

(smiles shyly)

Something's going on. Three of my batchmates have been asked to monitor professional dancing girls at bars.

RANI

Maybe they are planning a vice-squad raid.

LILY

(laughs)

Hardly. I've been on many a vice-squad raid. Takes about five minutes of planning. This is something big.

SCENE 20

Int. Night. Rani's bedroom.

Anzar nuzzling up to Rani and tickling her ear with the ends of her plait and kissing her on her neck.

RANI

What's to tell? It's a hackneyed feudal story. We were landed gentry. Super rich. My father was a philanderer, drunkard and gambler. We lost everything by the time I was nine. I intend to get it all back and plenty more. I'm never going to be poor again. End of story.

ANZAR

Just how do you plan to be a zillionaire?

RANI

Make good investments unlike the one I made in a certain fraud called Anzar.

ANZAR

What about the rest of the family?

RANI

I had a brother. On his fourteenth birthday he finished a full bottle of Scotch with three friends and drove the Jaguar over seven people sleeping on the pavement. Luckily, he managed to kill himself too. My mother was wise. She took off long before my father lost it all.

ANZAR

(unbuttoning her blouse)

What happened to you after you father died?

RANI

My father's sister and her husband took me in but I proved to be more than a handful. So they sent me to an orphanage.

A car starts honking. It's extremely loud and insistent. It's clear that Rani can't take the noise.

RANI

(melodramatically, deliberately like a Hindi movie heroine)

If you love me, you will make that man go out of his mind and curse the day he was born.

Anzar gets up, moves the window curtain and takes down the number of the car. As he does this, you can see the face of the man at the wheel.

ANZAR

Let me see what I can do.

SCENE 21

Int. Morning. Operations Room at the Police HQ.

A meeting of the senior brass of the Bombay police. There is a big map of Bombay on the wall and alongside it is a huge chart with the heading: Mafia–Dancing Girl nexus.

CHART

Rubaiyat Bar (Ballard Estate)

Bijlee-Salehbhai
Bijlee-Lal Ghulam
Bijlee-Raju Pawate

Raat Rani-Sattar
Raat Rani-Bada Rajan
Raat Rani-Karim
Raat Rani-Balu

Shangrila Bar (Ghatkopar)

Barkha-Rampyare
Barkha-Suleiman
Barkha-Ali

Shyama-Arun
Shyama-Salim

Mushaira Bar (Byculla)

Salma-Sahil
Salma-Dadu
Salma-Pagal Chhuri

Padmini-Randhva
Padmini-Ibrahim
Padmini-Purshottam

Madhbi-Garam Naram
Madhbi-Sanjay
Madhbi-Kalu Miya

Saaqui Bar (Koliwada, Sion)

Sangita-Bade Miyan
Sangita-Joshikaka
Sangita-Tiger

Lal Choli-Pasina Pasina
Lal Choli-Bhagwandada

Sawan-Murtaza
Sawan-Avinash
Sawan-Musharraf
Sawan-Zalim

REGINA

These are just four of the twenty bars we need to investigate.

DCP SHARMA

We've been at it for two months now but not one of those girls has talked.

DCP KHAN

Why would they want to betray their mafia clients? All it will earn them is a funeral.

DCP SHARMA

Take my word for it, you can never rely on them.

REGINA

Can they rely on us? Will you and I go out on a limb for them? Friendship is a two-way street.

DCP KHURANA

What kind of timeframe are we talking about?

Regina looks quietly at the others at the table.

REGINA

You really want to know? A lifetime. Those women are our best bet.
Don't work for the payoff. Only then the payoff may come our way.
Report to me in a week's time.

The other police officers are leaving when Regina's cell phone rings. She looks at the number.

REGINA

Hello. What a lovely surprise. Where are you?

PAWAN

At the Dorchester in London. The other half of the bed is empty.

REGINA

If only I could, I would take the flight tonight.

PAWAN

Just called to say I have filed the divorce papers.

REGINA

Are you sure? I'm happy to be with you just as we are.

PAWAN

I'm not.

REGINA

My ex-husband thought I was married not to him but to my job.
I hope you won't think that.

PAWAN

You forget that I'm out of the country half the time.
So it suits me fine.

REGINA

Love you, Pawan.

SCENE 22

Ext. Day. A school playground.

Behind the school building the kindergarten children are playing in the playground. There are various brightly coloured seesaws, slides with tunnels, low swings, and sandpits in which the children are having a whale of a time. Regina is standing with a camera (it's got a telephoto lens) behind the compound fence and is taking pictures. There's another camera around her neck. A good-looking woman in her mid-twenties comes and stands a little distance away from Regina. She has a child's lunchbox with her. She keeps looking at the children, especially one little boy and then turns to look at Regina who seems oblivious of her. The woman hesitates, then draws a little closer, though not too close to Regina. The woman's name is Bijlee. There's something vulnerable about her. She is wearing a green polyester-cotton sari with the pallu wrapped around her shoulders demurely. She wears pale lipstick and around the knot of her hair is a string of mogra flowers.

BIJLEE

(smiles and speaks with repressed pride)

The noisiest boy there, the one who's coming down the slide, is my son.

REGINA

(turns her head towards Bijlee, smiles, then looks at the boy and clicks)

Good-looking boy. Just like you. What's his name?

BIJLEE

Rajeev. Is your son here too?

REGINA

No. I don't have any children. I mean, not yet.

Bijlee looks a bit puzzled. Regina continues to shoot.

BIJLEE

Then why are you taking pictures of these children?

REGINA

I love shooting children. Their faces never lie.
You come here every day?

BIJLEE

Only when I am not too tired and sleepy.

REGINA

You work a night shift?

BIJLEE

(realizes that she's given more information than she intended)

No, I'm just too lazy.

The bell rings and Bijlee's son runs to his mother and hugs her.

RAJEEV

What have you got for lunch?

Rajeev realizes that his mother has company. He looks at Regina and clings to his mother even more. Regina now takes several pictures of mother and son together. She replaces the telephoto with a normal lens, takes a few more shots and then puts the cap back on the camera.

REGINA

I must be off.

She comes close to Rajeev and puts out her hand. Rajeev timidly takes it.

REGINA

Hello, Rajeev. *(He's too shy to respond.)* Bye now.

BIJLEE

I do work nights.

REGINA

I do too. Very often.

BIJLEE

(seems to grimace involuntarily)

I'm sure you don't do the kind of job I do. *(Regina is silent.)*
I'm a dancing girl at the Rubaiyat Bar.

REGINA

My name's Regina. What's yours?

BIJLEE

Bijlee.

Regina waves out to Bijlee as she leaves. In the shadow of the entrance to a building, Rani has been watching Regina and Bijlee talk.

SCENE 23

Int. Night. The Cyberia Café.

A man approaches Anzar, who's working at a computer. He waits for some time.

ANZAR

(without looking up)

What's on your mind?

FIRODIA

The word on the street is that there's a new kid on the IT block. And he's the best.

ANZAR

(looks up after a long time)

So?

SCENE 24

Int. Night. A dimly lit five-star restaurant.

Anzar and Firodia are having a meal at a quiet corner.

FIRODIA

I run a company called Internal Security Firewalls. ISF makes zero-tolerance security systems. Our target market is exclusively the Fortune 500 companies. As you can imagine, they already have the best security systems in place. However, as you know, even the best

systems are porous. Having spent millions, of course these companies are loath to believe it. But they are also terrified that someone might break in and steal their secrets.

Firodia looks at Anzar, waiting for a response.

ANZAR

Go on.

FIRODIA

Our job is to show these high-end companies that their internal systems are not failsafe.

ANZAR

Where do I figure in this?

FIRODIA

They say you can get in and out of anywhere. And you never leave any traces behind.

Firodia looks expectantly at Anzar, hoping that the latter will respond favourably to this lavish praise. But Anzar is poker-faced.

ANZAR

I'm still listening.

FIRODIA

We'll pay you on par with the best in the world. In dollars, of course.

ANZAR

But you're going against your own logic. Some new kid will turn up, crack my code and slip right in just as I might.

FIRODIA

Break in and I'll take care of the rest. *(Smiles and shrugs)* Naturally, you will sign a contract of confidentiality. You will work from home. This dedicated cellphone's for your calls. Keep them to the absolute minimum. If we must meet, I'll choose the place.

SCENE 25

Int. Night. A goldsmith's shop.

Rani watches as the goldsmith swiftly but with astounding craftsmanship turns the thinnest gauge gold wire into a filigreed miniature rosebud.

RANI

Is it done?

The goldsmith opens a drawer under the work table and puts the duplicate Vijayanagar set, necklace, earrings, bangles and cummerpatta on the table, without a word, along with the magazine picture of the set. Rani examines the pieces, ruby by fake ruby as well as the full setting with a very powerful magnifying glass. Finally, she raises her head.

RANI

Perfect. I couldn't tell the difference between the original and this one.

SCENE 26

Int. Day. The Maharani Suite at the Taj Mahal Hotel near the Gateway of India.

Rani is sitting in the drawing room. She's wearing a priceless heirloom of a sari. It is neither fussy nor ostentatiously expensive. Only those who know the real thing will understand how pricey and rare it is. Rani has her head covered with a pallu that's like an overhang and covers her forehead, eyes and much of her face. She wears a thin classic diamond necklace and matching earrings. She is what her name suggests, a princess. The effect is one of elegance and centuries of aristocratic breeding and bearing. The jeweller, Parshuramji, is, in his own way, a dignified elderly gentleman. He is sitting on a sofa behind a large table that has two leather cases on the side. The lid of one case is open, revealing very old traditional jewellery. Each case has four drawers, filled with exquisitely arranged pieces of expensive jewellery.

RANI

Thank you for coming. As you know, ours is a very traditional royal family and my mother, Her Highness, is in purdah and never appears in public. She hopes that you will respect these ancient customs.

Parshuramji is not awestruck but he's aware that he's in the presence of old royalty. Since the door of the adjoining room is open, he can see the silhouette of the Queen Mother sitting on the sofa in profile with her pallu drawn over her head.

PARSHURAMJI

Of course I understand. Please convey my gratitude to Her Highness for giving me this opportunity of showing her some very rare pieces.

RANI

It's best that I spell out at the outset how my family conducts business. *(Slight pause)* We do not make any payments. *(Parshuramji looks a bit startled.)* If Her Highness chooses any jewellery, her secretary will come over, negotiate the price, get the approval from us and will get back to you and make the payment. Does that suit you?

PARSHURAMJI

That would suit us perfectly.

Parshuramji places one of the carry-on cases on the glass table, opens the four drawers and lays one jewellery set after another on the table.

RANI

I've a fair idea of what Her Highness likes. So I will select some of the jewellery and present it to her.

Rani looks over the stuff, makes two trips to her mother to show her some of the jewellery exhibited. You can hear some soft conferring. She returns expressionless and places the jewellery back on the table. By the third trip, Parshuramji sees that the session is not going well.

RANI

Beautiful, but as I told you on the phone, Her Highness, Maharanisahiba, is interested in the Vijayanagar set which belonged

to our royal family and which her grandfather lost to the Nizam when they played the traditional game of cards on Lakshmipuja day.

PARSHURAMJI

(silent for a few moments)

Your Highness, when serving a meal, they say that the best should always be kept for the last.

Parshuramji carefully puts every item back in the case and then goes to the next one. He opens the bottom drawer and takes out a dark-red velvet box which has an unusual lining of bottle-green velvet. The aged jeweller knows exactly how rare the pieces he's about to show are. He looks at the princess and pauses for effect. And then opens the box to reveal an exquisite ruby necklace. You can hear the intake of the princess's breath. It is indeed a stunning and unusual piece. He proceeds to unveil the full ruby set: necklace, earrings, bangles, and cummerpatta. The princess walks towards her mother. Long shot from Parshuramji's perspective. Rani talks softly to the maharani. All you can hear is a murmur. She returns to the living room.

RANI

Her Highness's secretary, Rai Bahadur Hanumant Singhji, will come tomorrow morning and settle accounts.

PARSHURAMJI

Your Highness, Princess, I beg you not to take offence but I will have to take the set back with me.

RANI

(rising to her regal height but still not showing her face and speaking sternly)

There is nothing more precious to our royal family than our honour. Her Highness will take possession of the set only after you have received the full price which you will discuss with Hanumant Singhji.

PARSHURAMJI

I beg Your Highness to forgive me for presuming that you wanted to keep it overnight. My sincerest apologies to you and Maharaniji.

RANI

Apology accepted. Please examine all your wares closely before you leave.

PARSHURAMJI

That won't be necessary.

RANI

On the contrary. Examine every single piece carefully and only when you are satisfied that each one is the genuine article will you take leave of Her Highness.

PARSHURAMJI

(chastised)

Yes, your Highness. *(He examines the jewellery perfunctorily.)* Everything is in perfect order. May I take leave of Her Highness and Your Highness now?

RANI

Yes, you may go now.

Parshuramji bows low to Rani and even more so to the maharani and leaves, walking backwards. Rani sits down on the sofa, stretching her legs. She's tired. She suddenly stirs, goes to the door, checks if anybody is around, closes the door firmly and goes into the bedroom. She quickly pulls off the scarf that covers a cardboard cutout of a woman and folds the cloth. She then folds the cardboard several times and shoves it into her Gucci bag. Cut to Rani walking out of the hotel in a pair of trousers and a scarf around her head.

SCENE 27

Int. Day. Inside the concrete Old Woman's Shoe at Malabar Hill.

FIRODIA

How much more time do you think it will take to crack the firewall code?

ANZAR

Depends on how complicated the syntax is. Anywhere between one week and four. As I get familiar with the style of each programmer, the process will speed up.

SCENE 28

Int. Day. Regina's office.

REGINA

Let me understand this. The maharani stayed in the inside room while you sat in the living room of the suite?

PARSHURAMJI

Yes.

REGINA

And you never got to see her face?

PARSHURAMJI

No.

REGINA

How do you know she was even in the adjoining room?

PARSHURAMJI

I heard the princess talking to her.

REGINA

And you heard Her Highness replying?

PARSHURAMJI

Obviously. The princess couldn't have been talking to herself.

REGINA

Why not?

PARSHURAMJI

(about to say something but changes his mind)

You mean to say there was nobody in the room?

REGINA

It's possible, isn't it?

PARSHURAMJI

Are you telling me she made a fool of me?

REGINA

Let's just say she was very convincing.

PARSHURAMJI

I am seventy-one years old and it's never happened to me before. What happens now?

REGINA

We'll start investigating the theft. Please remember we are dealing with *(she pauses and smiles wryly)* the finest in the field.

PARSHURAMJI

I imagine this is going to be a difficult case.

REGINA

Yes.

PARSHURAMJI

She looked me in the eye the whole time I was there. And will you believe it, the princess insisted that I examine every piece before I left?

REGINA

Yes?

PARSHURAMJI

I did. I don't know how she did it but when I opened the box again in my office, there was a picture of a black flower there.

SCENE 29

Ext. Morning. Street

Rani and Anzar returning from a jog. They are about to enter the compound of her building when she spots the man in the Porsche who is

fond of blowing his horn. He merely touches the rim of the horn and the speakers in his car nearly knock him down with the horn playing at a ear-splitting volume. The man jumps up, screaming blue murder. He opens the door of his car and runs out, shaking and shattered. The noise subsides after half a minute. Everybody on the road is watching. He reopens the door, gingerly steps in closes the door and starts the car. He sees a line of cars in front, and blows the horn and screams, Fuck, fuck, fuck.

With every 'fuck', he hits the horn and the noise from the speakers keeps getting louder and louder.

RANI

(laughing her head off)

How did you do it, Anzar? I owe you one.

ANZAR

If anybody else's mad honking disturbs you, just give me the car number and the make of the car. I'll take care of him.

SCENE 30

Ext. Evening. A crowded street.

Rani, in jeans and a loose top, walking briskly. She stops at a shop that buys old newspapers, magazines and bottles. Rani waits for the previous customer to finish his transaction with the elderly businessman.

RANI

What's the price for old paper today?

SHOPKEEPER

(offhandedly)

Glossy or newsprint?

RANI

Newsprint.

SHOPKEEPER

(brusquely)

The rates are all there on the blackboard.

RANI

(goes over the rates)

I'll send my man with the papers.

SHOPKEEPER

Suit yourself.

SCENE 31

Ext. Evening. Lane next to the paper shop.

Rani leaves the shop and turns into the adjoining lane. She opens her handbag and takes out a hand mirror. She looks at herself, applies a touch of lipstick while simultaneously moving the mirror strategically to see if anyone's following her. She puts the mirror and the lipstick back, walks a little further and enters a building.

SCENE 32

Int. Evening. Inside the shopkeeper's home.

Noor Jehan, the daughter of the shopkeeper, welcomes Rani.

NOOR JEHAN

Come in, Raniji. Please sit down. My father called to say he'll be with you in a minute.

The house is an old spacious place that says old-world Muslim. You sit on the floor on fine carpets and mattresses covered with spotless white sheets.

RANI

What lovely bangles.

NOOR JEHAN

(pleased)

You like them? I got them in Hyderabad.

Noor Jehan rushes inside, gets a huge bangle box and shows off her bangles. She makes Rani try on the bangles. Abdulbhai, the old vendor who was rude to Rani a while ago at the shop, enters.

RANI

Salaam alequm, Abdulbhai.

ABDULBHAI

Walequm as-salaam.

ABDULBHAI

Beti, don't you want to look after our guest?

NOOR JEHAN

Forgive me, Abbajaan.

She goes in and returns with two tall glasses of lassi followed by kababs and other delicacies.

RANI

How are you, Abdulbhai?

ABDULBHAI

Allah has been kind. My only problem is my son. He hero-worships my son-in-law in Dubai.

RANI

Why is that a problem?

ABDULBHAI

My son-in-law Farhad is a fanatic and I fear for my son. But what about you, Ranisahiba?

RANI

Allah has been kind to me too.

ABDULBHAI

(to his daughter)

Beti, now leave us in peace till I call you. No phone calls either.

Rani opens her large bag, takes out the Vijayanagar set and lays each item gently on a very low table with a lamp attached to it. Abdulbhai looks at the pieces for some time, switches on the powerful light and takes a jeweller's lens out from his pocket. He goes over each piece thoroughly, ruby by ruby. Rani is far too much of an old hand to break the silence.

ABDULBHAI

(he never raises his voice and is not excitable)

This is good.

RANI

What's the market like?

ABDULBHAI

Not euphoric but steady. Besides, we never transact business unless the climate is just right. Have a kabab.

RANI

(picks up one and eats with relish)

The best kababs in the whole of Bombay.

ABDULBHAI

Where do you want the money? Switzerland or Luxembourg?

RANI

Luxembourg.

ABDULBHAI

Squeeze a little lemon juice on the kababs. They taste better.

SCENE 33

Int. Evening. Anzar's bedroom.

The room is bare except for an iMac, computer books on a shelf, a steel cupboard and a bed. Rani takes a rupee coin from behind Anzar's ear,

turns it into a shower of coins, then converts the coins into a twelve-foot-long scarf which she waves around and turns into a stick. Anzar gapes at Rani's magic tricks in sheer wonder and awe.

ANZAR

How do you do it?

RANI

Magic.

ANZAR

Show me.

RANI

Then it wouldn't be magic any longer.

Cut to Anzar leaning over and handing a contract on bond paper to Rani. Rani looks at the contract.

RANI

What is it?

ANZAR

The contract you wanted. Thirty-three per cent of everything I earn.

SCENE 34

Int. Day. Regina's office.

REGINA

She's a real pro. Didn't touch any of the other pieces. Held the velvet boxes but didn't touch the jewellery. She made Parshuramji examine every single piece she returned at the end.

DCP KHAN

No fingerprints, no violence, no leads.

REGINA

Would you pull out the records of Black Tulip's earlier robberies for me?

DCP KHAN

Which one?

REGINA

The lot.

DCP KHAN

(incredulous)

You sure?

REGINA

(sharply)

Of course, I am.

Cut to DCP Khan wheeling in a trolley piled up with files.

REGINA

What's that?

DCP KHAN

The Black Tulip files.

REGINA

You're joking.

DCP KHAN

No. There are a couple of hundred interviews, testimonies and interrogations.

SCENE 35

Ext. Late night. Outside Rubaiyat Bar.

Regina is sitting in a Toyota Innova parked inconspicuously, casing Rubaiyat Bar. She is dressed casually. Every now and then the door opens when a few latecomers go in or some people from inside leave and you hear loud Hindi film music. She makes sure there's no one outside Rubaiyat Bar and gets out of her car. She crosses the road and peers through the six-inch circular glass window on the wooden door. Customers

are eating and drinking at many of the tables. The last dance of the night is going on. The song is an old favourite: 'Parday mein rehne do, parda na uthao'. Seven girls in long skirts made from China silk and shiny plastic 'zari' thread and blouses with deep necklines decorated with sequins, mouth the song and gyrate their bodies provocatively. They are all tired but do their job as professionally as they can. Some of the customers get up from their tables, stick fifty-, hundred- and even five-hundred-rupee notes in the cleavages of the girls and use the opportunity to grope the women's breasts and buttocks.

CUSTOMER

(addresses Bijlee)

I booked you from the first song. Don't forget.

BIJLEE

And I told you someone else booked me seven days ago.

CUSTOMER

Bastard. How much is he paying you? I'll pay twice as much.

BIJLEE

Why don't you make a date for next Saturday? I'll give you the time of your life.

CUSTOMER

Time of my life? Promise? *(Pause)* No, I want you now.

SCENE 36

Ext. Late night. Outside Rubaiyat Bar.

The lights in Rubaiyat Bar go off and so does the neon sign. Bijlee is the first to emerge from the side entrance to the place. She walks hurriedly towards a cab while the customer continues to pursue her. He is drunk but not in the usual Hindi-film fashion. Regina has started the car and eases it towards Bijlee. She rolls the window down and calls out softly.

REGINA

Bijlee.

Bijlee has been too engrossed in walking away from the customer to notice the car coming abreast of her. She stops in fearful surprise. She looks into the window and places her hand on the window frame to steady herself.

BIJLEE

I thought it was Salehbhai.

Her eyes close in relief but now she looks even more flustered.

REGINA

Who's Salehbhai?

BIJLEE

(shakes her head)

Someone you never want to run into. Why have you come here, madam? I feel so ashamed.

REGINA

Get in, Bijlee.

BIJLEE

(hesitates, then gets in reluctantly since the man is pestering her)

Do you know how dangerous this place is? It's also illegal. What if something had happened to you?

REGINA

I went to Rajeev's school before lunch break for a week but neither you nor Rajeev was there.

BIJLEE

(calms down)

Rajeev's been having high fever.

REGINA

What does the doctor say?

BIJLEE

What they always say when they want to shut you up. Virus. But he's better today.

Regina puts her hand on Bijlee's for a second, then removes it a little self-consciously.

REGINA

I wanted to show you the pictures.

BIJLEE

(her face lights up even in the dark)

Rajeev's?

REGINA

Yours too.

BIJLEE

(shyly)

May I?

REGINA

In this light?

BIJLEE

(crestfallen)

Just drop me near a taxi.

REGINA

I'll drop you home and show you the pictures.

BIJLEE

No, you can't.

REGINA

Why not?

BIJLEE

It's a rathole.

REGINA

Think of me as a rat then.

They both laugh.

SCENE 37

Int. Late night. Bijlee's one-room place in a chawl.

Bijlee pays an elderly lady who has been looking after the child.

BIJLEE

(softly)

Did he get any sleep tonight?

ELDERLY LADY

Yes. And no fever, either.

BIJLEE

I'll see you tomorrow night, Laxmibai.

Elderly lady leaves. Bijlee immediately sets about straightening the room. Next to Rajeev's bed there are posters of cars stuck to the wall.

BIJLEE

Please sit. Will you have a cup of tea?

Regina sits down, shakes her head.

BIJLEE

A cold drink?

REGINA

(takes out the pictures from her bag and hands them to Bijlee)

Yes, thank you.

Bijlee pours out a Coke for her. Rajeev wakes up. Bijlee goes over to the bed and kisses him.

RAJEEV

What have you got for me?

BIJLEE

At this time of the night?

RAJEEV

Then why did you come back so late?

REGINA

I've got something for you.

Rajeev notices her and looks away shyly. Regina produces a gift-wrapped package. Rajeev is reluctant to take it.

REGINA

It's for you.

Rajeev unwraps the package. It's a model of a fancy BMW. Rajeev's eyes widen in amazement.

RAJEEV

It's a BMW. *(He looks up at the poster of Sachin Tendulkar.)* The same model that Sachin drives. Want to race?

REGINA

I don't have a car.

RAJEEV

You can have my old Mustang.

Regina and Rajeev skate the cars across the floor while Bijlee looks at the photographs.

BIJLEE

May I keep one?

REGINA

(looking up)

They are yours, the lot.

SCENE 38

Ext. Night. 'Natural Ice Cream' shop.

Anzar's wardrobe has improved considerably. Rani and Anzar are having an ice cream sitting at one of the tables outside the ice cream parlour. A police van with an insistent siren is coming their way.

RANI

How good are you?

ANZAR

You want to do it right here on the road?

RANI

You are the most concupiscent man I've met.

ANZAR

(his eyebrows dance)

I don't know what that word means but I like it.

Anzar licks the ice cream cone in an exaggerated fashion.

RANI

I was talking about hacking.

ANZAR

Pretty good. Why?

Rani's eyes seem to be still following the police van which has just gone by.

RANI

Wouldn't it be exciting to know just which baddies ACP Regina Fielding is after?

SCENE 39

Int. Night. Rani's drawing room.

A tight close-up of a man in a superbly fitted white suit.

MAN

We're talking six million dollars here. Three for you, three for me. Plus zero risk. You draw up a high-precision plan, every single detail in place and rob my casino. Half for you, half for me. Plus I get the insurance money.

The camera pans to another man now.

OTHER MAN

Thanks, Jack, but no thanks. You know I retired two years ago. I am done with my past life.

RANI

(Off-screen, but the voice is unmistakable.)

Give me a break!

Camera now on Rani and Anzar watching a film.

RANI

(mimicking sarcastically)

I'm retired. I'm done with my past life. Hardly any thief, big-time or small, retires. He can't. It's in his blood, an addiction. He has to keep pushing the envelope to get a high.

ANZAR

Wow. What makes you so sure?

RANI

You don't need to be a pop psychologist or Freud to know that. And yet every Hollywood heist film has the very same scene.

SCENE 40

Int. Late night. Bijlee's room.

Rajeev is fast asleep. Bijlee and Regina are having Scotch from the bottle that Regina has brought with her.

BIJLEE

Will you do me a favour?

REGINA

Depends on what you ask for.

BIJLEE

Please don't ever come here. Nor to Rubaiyat Bar.

REGINA

Why?

BIJLEE

Please don't ask.

REGINA

You want to break our friendship?

BIJLEE

Better that than a broken backbone.

REGINA

Would you like to come to my place?

BIJLEE

(looks horrified)

You are joking, right?

REGINA

No, I'm not.

BIJLEE

A dance girl in your home?

REGINA

It's a living.

BIJLEE

At least you try to be my friend.

REGINA

I am your friend.

BIJLEE

(smiling ruefully)

You are a cop.

SCENE 41

Int. Night. Anzar's bedroom.

Anzar is sitting at his computer. He has no clothes on. Rani is pulling her tank top down over her head.

RANI

For God's sake, get into some clothes.

ANZAR

Is this what you were looking for?

Rani bends down and reads the title in the left-hand corner of the computer screen: From: ACP Regina Fielding. *Rani looks wide-eyed and whistles.*

RANI

Mother of God. That's a crime, isn't it?

ANZAR

Hey, you asked me.

RANI

(still awestruck)

How did you do it?

ANZAR

(in his element now)

Any hacker with a little bit of brains can do it.

SCENE 42

Ext. Day. Outside Rajeev's school.

Bijlee appears tense as Rajeev eats his meal. Cut to Regina looking around carefully, then getting out of her car. She's in casuals.

REGINA

Hi, Rajeev. I've missed you. I've got something for you. You must promise me that you'll look at it only when you go home.

Rajeev is delighted to see Regina but he's still shy.
The school bell rings.

RAJEEV

Why not now?

REGINA

Now you know why.

RAJEEV

Can't I take it to class?

REGINA

You want to share it with everybody else?

Regina hugs Rajeev and kisses him on the cheek. Bijlee too kisses him hurriedly.

BIJLEE

Run or you'll be late.

Rajeev follows his mother's advice and runs. Bijlee looks distracted and preoccupied.

REGINA

What's on your mind, Bijlee? Can I help you in any way?

BIJLEE

(looking very troubled)

I don't know if I'm making a blunder.

REGINA

About what?

BIJLEE

Talking to you.

REGINA

Don't, if you're uncomfortable. Or if it's going to get you into trouble.

BIJLEE

(laughs bitterly)

I've been in trouble since I came to know Rajeev's father.

Regina looks puzzled.

BIJLEE

My first customer—Salehbhai.

Bijlee is about to say something more but changes her mind.

REGINA

Anything, absolutely anything you tell me would be invaluable. It's also 100 per cent confidential.

BIJLEE

That's all you are interested in, isn't it?

REGINA

It's my job to keep the people of this city safe.

BIJLEE

(looks stricken and then blurts out)

There's an illegal consignment of gold coming on a luxury liner docking tomorrow night.

REGINA

On a luxury liner?

BIJLEE

That's what I heard. More consignments are on the way.

REGINA

(whispers)

Why don't I provide police protection for you and Rajeev? Better still, come and stay with me.

BIJLEE

And what do I do when you are transferred? Besides, nowhere on this planet is safe when they are after you.

REGINA

I know you won't believe me but I *am* your friend.
Here's my address and personal phone number.
And my colleague Bilquis Khan's.

Bijlee shrugs.

SCENE 43

Ext. Day. A newspaper shop.

Rani buying an eveninger. The headline reads: 'ACP Regina Fielding sets record. Foils third shipment of illicit gold.' *Cut to…*

Ext./Int. Day. Anzar's room.

Anzar opens the door, sees Rani outside.

ANZAR

What have you got for me?

RANI

Is that all that you are interested in?

ANZAR

Yes.

Anzar abruptly closes the door. When he opens it again, she's gone.

ANZAR

Damn. Rani, wait, wait. I love you. I love you more than the moon, the sun, Saturn, Jupiter, Neptune, Pluto and all that zodiac horseshit put together. Come back. Come back.

No sign of Rani. Anzar runs down the stairs barefoot. He's hardly reached the first landing when Rani comes out from where she's hiding behind his open door, gets in and slams the door hard. Anzar hears the door, rushes up and rings the bell.

RANI

Who's there?

ANZAR

The love of your life. Open the door.

RANI

Not unless you've got something for me.

ANZAR

I have, I have.

RANI

Swear.

ANZAR

I swear on my Hindu mother and Muslim father.

RANI

(letting him in)

Where's the present?

ANZAR

Oh, I lied.

RANI

(hitting him all over)

You'll pay for this.

ANZAR

(making all kinds of noises of pleasure)

Ooh. Aaaahhh. More please. More. I'll buy a leather thong and leather boots and a whip.

Anzar hands Rani a sealed envelope.

RANI

What's in it?

Rani tears open the envelope.

ANZAR

Money to buy the leather stuff.

RANI

A cheque for two hundred thousand and ninety rupees? Are you in on the gold shipments?

ANZAR

I had no idea you can't read.

RANI

What are you talking about? Two hundred and ninety thousand rupees. *(Long pause)* My God, dollars.

SCENE 44

Int. Day. The Operations Room at the Police HQ.

DCP Khan and DCP Sharma are chatting away when Regina enters to a chorus of greetings. She acknowledges the greetings perfunctorily but it's evident that something's wrong.

DCP KHAN

Congratulations.

REGINA

I thought we had an agreement that not a word about informants was to be mentioned to the press.

DCP SHARMA

We've done our job. The public has the right to know.

REGINA

I take the decisions here, DCP Sharma. Is that clear? The job has not even begun. The idea was to make sure that the underworld doesn't feel a loss of face.

DCP PANDE

Why worry about what they feel?

REGINA

Because they might feel the need to teach us a lesson.

DCP SHARMA

(cocky and challenging)

Are you afraid of them?

REGINA

(quiet and cold, looking Karan Sharma in the eye)

Yes. *(Pause)* I'm always afraid for the lives and property of our citizens as I am for your life and mine. And most of all, I'm afraid for my informant.

SCENE 45

Int. Night. Regina's apartment.

Regina's phone rings.

REGINA

Hello. Regina Fielding. Hello?

BIJLEE

(off-screen)

Madam, this is Bijlee.

REGINA

Hello, Bijlee. Are you all right?

BIJLEE

Tomorrow at 3 a.m. at Danda beach.

(Sound of line getting cut off.)

REGINA

Hello? Hello? Bijlee?

SCENE 46

Ext. Late night. Danda beach.

A posse of policemen and officers in mufti are positioned at different points on Danda beach, in fishing boats and amongst the trees. Five

others, including Regina, also in mufti, are keeping a watch from behind boats parked on the sands. Regina looks at her watch. It's 3 a.m., then 4, then 5. Regina's cellphone registers an SMS. 'Thank you for keeping a watch, Reginabai, but the stuff was delivered at Versova beach at 3 a.m. sharp.'

REGINA

Oh shoot! We've been had. Oh God, no. Are you all right, Bijlee?

Regina dials a number. The auto response voice recording comes on. 'The number you are trying to reach is either switched off or out of reach.'

SCENE 47

Int. Dawn. Outside Bijlee's house.

Regina knocks on Bijlee's door. No sound. Regina knocks again a little louder and longer this time.

REGINA

(softly)

Bijlee, open the door, it's me, Regina. *(Waits for a response.)*

REGINA

Please, Bijlee. I've got a toy for Rajeev.

Laxmibai, the neighbour who looks after Rajeev, opens the door next to Bijlee's.

LAXMIBAI

Why are you yelling? *(She sees it's Regina and her tone changes.)* Don't bother, madam. She's not there.

REGINA

Isn't she back from work?

LAXMIBAI

No. She went out with some people last evening.

REGINA

Where's Rajeev?

LAXMIBAI

She took him too.

SCENE 48

Int. Dawn. Regina's apartment.

Bilquis Khan shows Regina the SMS on her cell phone: Save my Rajeev. Please. *Regina rises from her chair instantly, puts on her cap and is already running down the stairs.*

REGINA

Has the cellphone company told us the location yet?

DCP KHAN

Reay Road. Next to the abandoned Unilever factory. I've asked for two back-up vans. *(hesitantly)* Ma'am, it's very likely a set-up.

REGINA

I'm sure. But what choice do we have? Ask the two back-up vans to wait round the corner for my instructions.

Cut to Regina's car speeding. No screeching breaks, Regina is a fine driver and the effect is of concentration and not of a Hollywood chase. It's a look at Mumbai just as dawn is about to break. Smog. The street lights render the atmosphere hazy. People lying helter-skelter on the pavement, covered and uncovered. A man pulling up a woman's sari as he's about to mount her. Posh high-rise buildings next to grimy chawls and lean-tos. The amber traffic lights keep flickering. Everything goes past in a blur. Regina makes a U-turn, heads back on another road and turns left. The sun will rise any moment. Headlights catch a battered Bijlee lying crumpled on the ground and Salehbhai standing next to her, dressed in a white embroidered polyester-cotton kameez and loose white trousers that narrow down at the ankles. Salehbhai has his arms up in the air. Behind him in the waters, a little bit away is a small yacht. Regina bends down to pick up Bijlee.

SALEHBHAI

Uh-ah. No touching. *(Regina stands up straight again.)* I am unarmed. Want to feel me up? *(Laughs)* My son's on the boat. *(Points to Bijlee.)* She calls him Rajeev. But his name's Alla Rakha. *(The lights from the yacht come on blindingly and you see armed men pointing their AK-47s at Regina)* How come you went to the wrong beach?

REGINA

Let Bijlee and your son go, Salehbhai. Let them have a normal life.

SALEHBHAI

I have every intention of letting her go.

Salehbhai bends down and picks Bijlee up. You see her bruised and battered face. He pulls her head back and runs an old-fashined cut-throat razor across her neck. The blood spurts out.

SALEHBHAI

There, she's gone.

He drops her to the ground. One of Salehbhai's goons is holding a gun to Rajeev's head.

SALEHBHAI

Tell your officers to hold their fire. You don't want any harm to come to my heir apparent. *(He walks up the plank to the boat and waves goodbye.)* Khuda hafeez, Madam. *(Receives an SMS and reads it.)* Tch, tch, tch, just got a message. You're losing your touch, Reginabai. Three simultaneous bank robberies while you're wasting your time here. I'm moving to Dubai. I'm going to miss you.

The yacht sputters and recedes. A red streak of flamingoes flies past the sun. It is a ravishing sight and then the camera pans over the bloody pool around Bijlee's slit throat.

SCENE 49

Int. Day. DGP Goray's office.

DGP GORAY

I brought you here because we have a crime wave on hand and I wanted results. Did I make a mistake, ACP Fielding? I'm getting flak from every quarter. We still don't know who's behind these bank robberies.

REGINA

It looks like they had access to inside information, sir. They knew the layout and every single detail. In all three places it appears they even had the diagram and code of the central safe.

DGP GORAY

Is Salehbhai the brains behind it?

REGINA

That's the market rumour but I've still got to question another thirty-two senior clerks and officers.

DGP GORAY

Wrap it up fast. If the ISI is behind the robberies, we'll have to inform the central government.

SCENE 50

Int. Morning. Rani's flat.

Rani, at her laptop, clicks on Regina's inbox and then clicks on an email from DGP Goray who has forwarded the mail he has received from DGP Delhi to her

RANI

(reads)

For DGP Goray's eyes only. See if you can decode this Interpol message: Let's watch three more films: Let's do the Dylan film called *I'm Not There* next Monday. And then *Chitty Chitty Bang Bang* on

Thursday. And *About A BOY* Monday week. Dinner and drinks on the house for the first film. And in case you've forgotten, my home's downtown just off Convent Street in Colaba. Most likely we'll do the second film at Salim's home on A.K. Road, Andheri East, and the last one at Abbas's place at Amba Bhavan in Sion West.

Cut to…

Rani has a set of Scrabble letters in three groups. BOB DYLAN. I'M NOT THERE. CHITTY CHITTY BANG BANG. ABOUT A BOY.

RANI

If he's inviting his friends over, why does he have to mention where he stays? And that too, without really giving the address?

She keeps arranging and rearranging the letters in various ways and keeps shaking her head. Gradually, she reduces the number of words so that she's left with BOB. CHITTY CHITTY BANG BANG. BOY. Now she adds some letters to BOB and comes up with Bank of Baroda. Then Citi Bank. And Bank of India.

SCENE 51

Ext. Noon. Rani casing different BOB branches in the Fort area.

Cut to ground floor of Bank of Baroda, Convent Street. Rani is standing in a queue at a counter and surveying the field. She finds herself at the head of the queue facing the person behind the counter.

RANI

(momentarily flummoxed)

Er… *(She realizes her mistake)* I mean, I want a form.

PERSON AT THE COUNTER

You want to open an account?

RANI

Yes.

Cut to Rani going round to the back of the building.

SCENE 52

Ext. Day. Outside Bank of Baroda.

The street theatre group including Rani, and other members performing in front of the Bank of Baroda branch at Kala Ghoda. Lily Pinto in uniform is watching. It's a tableau of the three monkeys. The first has her eyes closed. The second member has her hands clamped around her ears and the third has her hands shutting her mouth.

A MEMBER OF THE GROUP

(singing)

Aakhein ho ke bhi andhe
Kaan hote bhi beherein
Mooh hote bhi goonge
Kaun Ram, kaun haram?
Aakhein khol ke dekho
Kaan hai to suno
Mooh hain to awaaz uthao.

Rani moves away and fixes her cellphone so that whoever receives her call will register 'caller unknown'. There's a queue of people waiting to be let into the BOB building. From her vantage point, Rani has a clear view of the door and the pavement across. The street theatre group continues to sing lustily. An armoured BOB van with steel plates covering its windows comes in from the Indira Docks end and pulls up at the BOB building. Four people in overalls stamped 'BOB' on their backs get out of the van and climb the steps. Rani, who is wearing a fashionable multi-pocketed pair of trousers, lags behind, crosses the road and stands on the pavement across from the BOB building. The van waits with its engine idling a little ahead of Rani. Rani pretends to count some change when a coin falls and rolls on the road. Rani bends down to pick it up. Camera cuts to a close-up of Rani's hand placing a small steel plate with a set of sharp, heavy-duty spikes under the front edges of the two wheels of the van on her side of the pavement. Rani now goes to a phone booth a few feet away from her. She dials 100 for the police.

RANI

Hello, Police? Emergency. Emergency. Robbery under way at Bank of Baroda, Convent Street Branch.

SCENE 53

Ext. Day. Opposite the BOB building.

RANI'S VOICE

(using her cellphone and mimicking Regina's voice)

Can you hear me, Sub-Inspector Lily Pinto?

LILY

(off-screen)

Sub-Inspector Lily Pinto. Who's calling?

RANI

ACP Regina Fielding

Intercuts between Sub-inspector Lily Pinto on the phone and Rani watching her from behind the van.

RANI

Robbery under way in Bank of Baroda premises. In a minute four people in BOB uniforms will come out and proceed to the silver armoured Mahindra Xylo van across the road near the Bank of Baroda building. Do not, I repeat, do not do anything till the van starts. It will come to a screeching halt. Now if anyone tries to get out of the van, shoot. I'll be there within three minutes with reinforcements. Good luck.

Cut to the robbers rushing out with loaded BOB bags and guns in their hands. The doors of the van are slammed shut and the van takes off instantly since the engine has been running throughout but it suddenly weaves drunkenly as two tyres suffer multiple punctures. The van is still trying to escape but is not making much progress. The leader who's sitting in the front next to the driver alights as Lily Pinto springs into the middle of the road, her gun at the ready.

LILY PINTO

Don't move or I'll shoot.

LEADER

Shoot, pig.

He aims at her chest and shoots but Lily Pinto dodges the bullet as she's waiting for this very move. She falls to the ground and pumps two bullets, one aimed at his hand and the other into his right thigh. In the meantime, police cars with sirens going full blast converge upon the van. The rear door of the van opens and the four other gangsters try to make a run for it while shooting wildly but Regina is waiting for them at the Indira Docks end. The leader of the gang halts a cab with his gun. He's about to get in when DCP Sharma yells at him. Rani runs around, taking care of those hurt in the random shooting.

DCP SHARMA

Don't even try.

Gang leader is about to close the door when a bullet pierces his stomach. Cut to gang leader being taken away in an ambulance along with the four handcuffed gangsters and the driver in a police van. Cut to Regina about to climb the robbers' van to survey the loot. She sees a note stuck to the door of the van. 'Congratulations'. *Under the note is the drawing of a black tulip.*

REGINA

(muttering to herself)

What devious game are you playing, Black Tulip?

Cut to the press interviewing Lily Pinto.

SUB-INSPECTOR PINTO

I just did my duty. ACP Fielding called me and told me what to do. She knew exactly what was going to happen.

SCENE 54

Int. Day. Regina's office.

REGINA

You have a cellphone?

SUB-INSPECTOR PINTO

Yes, ma'am.

REGINA

Did you see my cellphone number when I was supposed to have called?

SUB-INSPECTOR PINTO

There was no number.

REGINA

My voice sounded the same as now?

SUB-INSPECTOR PINTO

Yes, I think so.

REGINA

Weren't you supposed to be on duty?

SUB-INSPECTOR PINTO

(looking sheepish)

From twelve o' clock, Ma'am. I just thought I would be with my theatre group before reporting for work.

REGINA

Who else was there with you?

SUB-INSPECTOR PINTO

(shrugs)

There were eleven or twelve of us. Rehana Ali, Felix D'sa, Agnes Pereira, Rani Agarkar, Arnanwaz Modi, Santan Saldhana, Ossie Lobo...

REGINA

Please give me a list of their names and telephone numbers.

SUB-INSPECTOR PINTO

Hindus, Muslims, Parsis … we're a mixed crowd.

SCENE 55

Int. Night. DGP Goray's office.

DGP GORAY

Do we finally have a grip on who's the kingpin behind these bank robberies?

REGINA

I've questioned twelve of the culprits so far and they all claim to be working for Salehbhai. But something's not quite right. Every one of them mouths the same story word for word.

DGP GORAY

Curious, isn't it?

REGINA

What's even more puzzling is that they know their Holy Book chapter and verse. But they are clueless about normal Muslim life.

DGP GORAY

Get to the bottom of this. Fast.

REGINA

I have been tracking one woman for months now. I think she is the brains behind this operation. I hope I will have news for you pretty soon.

DGP GORAY

There's something else. I want you to upgrade the IT crimes department to state-of-the-art. You will have a free hand. Preferably use the talent within the force itself. Industrial espionage is the fastest-growing criminal activity here and internationally. It's valued in billions, perhaps trillions.

REGINA

I'm not exactly a wizard with computers, sir.

DGP GORAY

Ferret out at least a few of the most seasoned and devious hackers. Give them a choice. They can go to jail. Or join us. Our techies go abroad and become billionaires. I want the Industrial Espionage division to be our biggest foreign exchange earner.

SCENE 56

Int. Afternoon. Inside the Bank of Baroda conference room.

Throughout this interrogation Regina is deliberately goading Ms Sathe, a woman of stern disposition in her mid-forties, to elicit information from her.

REGINA

Are you married, Mrs Sathe?

Ms SATHE

I'm single.

REGINA

How many children?

Ms SATHE

I just told you I'm not married.

REGINA

So what? We live in modern times. India's changing.

Ms SATHE

You may be living in godless times but I'm not.

REGINA

How many years have you been working in the Bank of Baroda?

Ms SATHE

Twenty-six.

REGINA

Wow, you must be loaded. I believe officers are paid very well.

Ms SATHE

Nowhere near what you corrupt policemen and women make on the side.

REGINA

So what are you going to do with all that money?

Ms SATHE

None of your business.

REGINA

I was wondering why you have been withdrawing such large sums of money after all these years. And that too, in cash.

Ms SATHE

I have relatives who need help.

REGINA

The only family you have is you. Unless you've acquired a fancy toyboy.

Ms SATHE

I'm a woman of principles. I'm a Hindu and am willing to die for my faith. It's filthy folks like you who we intend to wipe out from our country.

REGINA

So you see yourself as the dispenser of the vengeance of God.

Ms SATHE

There are thousands of other committed Hindus like me who won't sit and watch the Pakis destroy our great country.

REGINA

You and your colleagues at Apakarat Apakaram decided to frame Salehbhai for bank robberies that your organization committed. You provided the complex code to the bank safe.

Ms SATHE

Since our spineless leaders won't do their job, we had no choice.

REGINA

The stolen money would finance and train Hindu mujahedeen to wreak vengeance and wipe out as many innocent Pakistanis as possible. And perhaps start a nuclear war.

MS SATHE

Any sacrifice for our motherland is worth it.
Vande Mataram. Jai Hind.

SCENE 57

Int. Morning. Rani's flat.

Rani's at the computer. She has accessed Regina's email. She reads to herself softly.

RANI

Dear Regina, Arriving Friday 7.30 pm. See you at the Taj. Can't wait to be in your arms. Love, Pawan.

SCENE 58

Ext. Evening. Nariman Point.

Anzar and Firodia opposite the NCPA at the end of the walkway. They're behaving like strangers. Lots of regulars are walking on the pavement.

ANZAR

I've done three assignments for you already and broken through all three firewalls. Who will know better than I how to come up with new impregnable firewalls?

FIRODIA

You forget we have no say in the matter. That's the condition they lay down in their contracts. Their experts join our team and supervise every single detail.

ANZAR

I'm the best in the field, you know that.

FIRODIA

You may be right but they cough up the moolah,
so they have the final say.

SCENE 59

Int. Evening. Corridor of the Taj Mahal Hotel.

Regina knocks on the door of a suite in the Taj Mahal Hotel in Bombay. Pawan opens the door. Pawan is in his early forties. He's good-looking, dresses in designer clothes and exudes the kind of confidence and easy manners that can only come from old money and a habit of power. Regina comes in and Pawan closes the door. As she proceeds, Pawan turns her around and grabs her. Regina is taken aback but responds warmly.

REGINA

You sure you want to go ahead with the divorce?

PAWAN

Yes.

REGINA

And the children?

PAWAN

You'll be a better mother to them than their own mother is.

REGINA

I can only try. But I don't want you to regret anything later on. *(Pause)* I'm happy to be with you … whenever you have the time.

PAWAN

(smiles)

I'm not. I want you round-the-clock.

(He hugs her again. Dissolve.)

SCENE 60

Int. Morning. Rani's flat.

Lily Pinto ringing the bell of Rani's apartment. Lily has a beautifully gift-wrapped package for Rani.

RANI

(opening the door)

Hey, what a surprise. You've become even more rare than an Eid ka chand.

LILY

Merry Christmas.

RANI

Merry Christmas to you too. *(Opens the package)* A pudding, a pudding, my kingdom for a Christmas pudding. *(Rani hugs Lily. Cut to Rani's dining room)* Where have you been?

LILY

I've got news for you.

RANI

You're getting married.

LILY

The IT Crimes division has been revamped and I'm one of its new faces. We've been on a four-month crash course in advanced IT crime tracking and I am now a full-fledged inspector.

RANI

Congratulations. We're going have dinner at the Thai Pavillion this Sunday to celebrate.

Cut to Rani and Lily at the Thai Pavillion.

SCENE 61

Int. Evening. The Thai Pavillion.

RANI

Here's a little something to show you how proud I'm of you.

Rani hands Lily a gift-wrapped box. Lily opens it and can't suppress her joy. It's a big gold cross.

LILY

For me? You can't give me such an expensive present.

RANI

(suddenly fake serious)

Show me the chapter and clause in the law. *(Pause)* Just wear it and you'll never go wrong.

SCENE 62

Ext. Day. On the 51st storey of the skeleton of a building looking out on to the sea.

RANI

(clinging to Anzar)

Are you going to stay so high up?

ANZAR

(walking around)

Not me. We.

RANI

What makes you so sure I'm going to move in with you?

ANZAR

This is your room. You won't hear a single car horn.

RANI

You didn't answer my question?

ANZAR

What question?

RANI

About moving in with you?

ANZAR

(sits on the floor, absent-minded)

You would rather not?

RANI

I'm keeping my apartment just in case you take three more wives.
What's bothering you, Anzar?

ANZAR

Nothing.

RANI

Out with it.

ANZAR

I'm making so much money, it's coming out of my ears.
But I get no satisfaction.

RANI

Why?

ANZAR

I always end up doing only half the job.

RANI

Why is that?

ANZAR

Because my employer says those are the rules of the game.

SCENE 63

Int. Night. DGP Goray's office.

DGP GORAY

You have good news for me?

REGINA

(hesitant)

I don't know whether it's good or bad, sir. Have you heard of an organization called Apakarat Apakaram.

DGP GORAY

All I know is those words mean tit for tat.

REGINA

That makes sense. These Hindutva extremists want *fittamphat.* They wish to destabilize our neighbour to the northwest.

DGP GORAY

I thought the Pakistanis have been doing that pretty well themselves.

REGINA

These people think the Indian government is gutless. They want to go to war every time there's an incident at the border.

DGP GORAY

Oh, for the good old days when heists were about money and not about fanatic retaliation. Good work, Regina.

REGINA

Thank you, sir.

DGP GORAY

(calls out as she's about to leave)

Just make sure the case against them is watertight. The extremists on either side will do their best to discredit you.

SCENE 64

Int. Morning. Rani's study.

Rani's on the computer accessing Regina's email. She clicks on the inbox and reads from the computer screen:

Dear Regina,

Congratulations. The foreign papers say you've avoided a full-scale war between the two countries.

Meet you at the Lake Palace Hotel on the 27th. It's off-season and we'll have almost the whole hotel to ourselves. Our honeymoon will start before our wedding.

Love,
Pawan

SCENE 65

Ext. Morning. Outside Santa Cruz airport.

ANZAR

(getting out of a cab with Rani)

You're abandoning me for a full four days?

RANI

Yes.

ANZAR

May I join you?

RANI

No. *(Conspiratorially)* The idea is to get away from you, stupid.

ANZAR

What will I do for sex?

RANI

Get an inflatable plastic doll. Or you could try and make more money. You've got a high-maintenance girlfriend.

ANZAR

I'm sure you've got a secret assignation with someone.

RANI

Not just one person. The whole Pakistani cricket team.

SCENE 66

Int. Day. The Lake Palace Hotel in Udaipur.

Regina and Pawan in a huge bathtub together.

REGINA

Oh to be in your arms in the Lake Palace for ever and ever and never have to think of work and all the racketeers, crooks and murderers in the city.

PAWAN

Seven days of this obscene luxury and you'll be bored out of your mind.

REGINA

Try me. At the end of seven years, I'll be begging you to let me stay for another seventy.

PAWAN

(makes a funny face)

What time do we go sightseeing?

REGINA

(gets up and nibbles at his ear and whispers)

We are not getting out of bed for at least a week.

Cut to Regina and Pawan in a lovely canopied boat drifting in Pichola Lake, which houses the Lake Palace Hotel.

SCENE 67

Ext. Day. The Eklingji Temple.

As Regina and Pawan are getting into the temple, some ragged beggars and urchins touch their clothes and tug at their hands. Regina quietly shooes them away while Pawan gets more and more worked up. The children are filthy and snot-nosed and can get really obnoxious. At one point, Pawan is about to cuff one of them when Regina grips his hand.

REGINA

No, Pawan.

PAWAN

I want to go back.

REGINA

(looks at him in surprise and dismay)

Go back?

PAWAN

Oh, don't be so dramatic. To the hotel.

SCENE 68

Int. Night. The Indian restaurant in the Lake Palace Hotel.

Regina and Pawan are having dinner. It's heavy-going since Pawan is sulking and hostile with suppressed resentment. Rani's sitting at another table behind, a little to the left of Regina. Regina can't see her but Rani has a good view of Pawan and can see Regina's profile. She can also hear their conversation.

REGINA

It's not the beggars and the urchins, is it, Pawan? *(Pawan keeps mum.)* What is it?

PAWAN

I've been trying to tell you something for the last two days but I can't seem to find the words. *(Regina is listening but won't help him along.)* I still can't.

REGINA

Shall I say it for you? *(Pawan looks at her, bemused.)* You want to break off.

PAWAN

How did you know?

REGINA

One always knows, doesn't one, though one pretends not to.

PAWAN

I tried, I did. I honestly did, Regina.

REGINA

I know you did.

PAWAN

I love you so. I'll die without you but … but I can't leave the children.

REGINA

I know. *(Pause)* Don't worry, you'll live.

Cut to the bell boy placing Pawan's luggage in the boat. Rani watches from the window of her room as Pawan tries to kiss Regina but she smiles enigmatically and steps back.

PAWAN

Won't you forgive me?

REGINA

You must ask that of your wife now.

(The boat leaves. Camera lingers on Regina standing all alone as the sun sets behind her.)

SCENE 69

Ext. Day. A Honda City with the hotel logo, at the edge of the lake.

Rani is sitting in one corner of the back seat. Regina gets out of the boat, climbs the steps. The driver opens the rear door for her.

REGINA

I'm sorry I kept you waiting. I didn't want to go to Chittor but the trip was on the hotel as an off-season bonus. So I said, why not? No point rotting in the room. *(Rani, shrinking further into herself, shrugs.)* Sorry, why am I bothering you with my chatter.

Throughout the journey to Chittor, Rani sits looking out of her window and Regina out of hers. Both of them continue to be uncommunicative but every now and then Rani surreptitiously watches Regina.

SCENE 70

Int. Day. At the top of Rana Kumbha's Victory Tower at Chittor.

There are four magnificent views of the fort and the various temples and structures from the four sides of the room on the top floor. Rani and Regina are standing away from each other at different windows on either side of the room. Rani is about to jump out when Regina quietly pulls her back.

REGINA

What are you doing?

RANI

Why don't you mind your own business?

REGINA

Come on. It can't be all that bad.

RANI

How would you know?

Regina takes a deep breath. It's against her grain to reveal anything about herself to anybody but on this occasion she makes an exception.

REGINA

Because a man just walked out on me after five-and-a-half years. I moped in my room for two days. This morning I swore I won't permit anyone else to ruin my life.

RANI

Five-and-a-half years? Men are swines. I hate them.

REGINA

Do you really? If you did, you'd get yourself a life, not kill yourself.

RANI

I loved him so. But I discovered after we got here that he was carrying on with another woman.

REGINA

This is not the first time someone's ditched me. I was married once.

RANI

What happened?

REGINA

He said I was married to my job, not to him.
He wanted a full-time wife.

RANI

What kind of job do you do?

REGINA

I'm with the police.

SCENE 71

Int. Night. At the bar in the Lake Palace Hotel.

Regina and Rani drinking at a table.

RANI

Do you love him very much?

REGINA

He always said he couldn't live without me. That should have warned me. What does your friend do?

RANI

My former friend. He thinks he's billionaire material.

REGINA

Is he?

RANI

I hope so. I have a thirty-three-and-a-half per cent stake in his company. *(Rani again slips into a morose expression.)*

REGINA

Maybe he'll realize his mistake and come back to you.

RANI

Sure. Like your man will fly back over the weekend.

REGINA

If only he would.

RANI

What does he do?

REGINA

Let's just say he was born a billionaire and is trying to make it to the trillionaire bracket.

SCENE 72

Int. Day. Near the Maharaja's Palace in Udaipur.

Rani and Regina at a crowded roadside ice cream parlour. Everybody at the shop is standing with mountainous toppings of ice creams on cones. Rani is holding her ice cream cone in one hand.

RANI

How much?

MAN AT COUNTER

Hundred and twenty.

Rani takes out two hundred-rupee notes from her wallet with her right hand and puts the wallet back into the leather bag that hangs from her shoulder. The man shortchanges her and the two of them have an altercation.

RANI

You gave me only fifty.

MAN AT COUNTER

You don't know how to count.

Rani counts.

MAN AT COUNTER

I bet you pocketed thirty.

He hands her Rs 30. Rani's taking the money when she suddenly screams.

RANI

My purse, my purse. Someone's stolen my purse.

SCENE 73

Int. Day. A police station in Udaipur.

Rani and Regina at the police station. Rani sits like a zombie.

POLICE OFFICER

(officiously reads from FIR)

You lost: Cash: Rs.3,000. Air ticket. Visa Infinity Card. Right? Sign.

RANI

(muttering, shaking her head in disbelief)

They stole from me? Me?

POLICE OFFICER

We'll call you at the hotel if we find anything.

Rani signs and her shoulders slump in dejection. Regina touches her elbow. Rani looks up.

REGINA

Come. *(Rani looks blank. Regina turns to police officer.)* What are the chances of finding the stolen stuff?

POLICE OFFICER

(even more officiously)

Who knows? Udaipur's a big city.

SCENE 74

Int. Night. Anzar's apartment.

ANZAR

(working on the desktop)

Go ahead, Mr Firodia. Work with your client and the best team in the world to design a new firewall. I will show you that I can break through it.

Dissolve to …

ANZAR

(still at the desktop)

I don't get it. Still no new firewall to replace the ones I've breached. Something fishy here. Mr Firodia, let's see what you've got to say. I'm going to record all incoming and outgoing calls on your phone from now on.

SCENE 75

Ext. Day. The same place where Rani was robbed.

Rani has spread out a mirror-work piece of cloth on the ground. She's in a leotard and is wearing coloured beads around her neck and wrists and is doing some amazing yogic asanas. A small crowd has begun to gather around her and a few people are dropping notes and coins into the

tambourine she's using as a bowl. Regina looks at her, spellbound. Rani now ties the dazzlingly exotic mirror-work cloth around her waist as a skirt, picks up the change, puts it in a mirror-work bag and uses the tambourine as an accompanying instrument. She starts to sing Hindi film songs in her lusty voice and dances with great verve. The crowd is growing. Rani uses her body and voice to great effect. A French hippie flower girl carrying a guitar joins in the busking. The crowd is clapping madly now. Rani is swirling away. Suddenly, Rani breaks off and in a trice is next to a local girl who has lifted a wallet from an American woman's handbag and passed it on. Rani holds the thief's hand in a vice-like grip. The woman yells and screams and thrashes around. The man who has been standing close to her has taken off with the wallet. Regina is now beside Rani.

RANI

Hold her.

Regina holds on to the woman while Rani shoots like a bullet to the ice cream shop where she slams hard into the man who had just left from among the spectators. The man sprawls on the ground but Rani has in the meantime leapt over the counter and knocked a fat wallet out of the hands of the man who served her at the ice cream parlour. Two policewomen are there by now and are trying to overpower Rani. One of them cuffs her on the jaw while the other handcuffs her. Meanwhile, Regina arrives at the scene with the thief and the American woman whose wallet has been stolen. The gang of thieves, including the man working at the ice-cream parlour, are behaving like highly aggrieved innocents. The American woman takes her driving licence and plastic cards out of the wallet that Rani is still hanging on to and shows them to the two policewomen. Regina pulls out her Bombay Police identification, dials the Udaipur police HQ and starts talking to the Commissioner of Police. The policewomen now release Rani.

AMERICAN WOMAN

Awesome. You're some dancer. And you're a real detective.

Rani is whizzing all over the inside of the shop, opening drawers, cupboards, doors and the cash register. She looks into the trash can. It's full of trash. Rani picks it up. It seems unusually heavy. Rani empties it in front of everybody. It stinks but by now five wallets are on the ground.

AMERICAN WOMAN

How did you know?

Rani is still not satisfied and ransacks the wooden drawers holding steel vessels containing different flavours of ice cream. She finds her wallet there. She goes through her stuff; the plastic and cash are missing.

REGINA

It won't be very long before we find the other missing items. The Superintendent of Police will be here in a moment.

SCENE 76

Ext. Day. In the Lake Palace motorboat.

Regina and Rani are going back to the hotel.

REGINA

How in God's name did you catch them?

RANI

(shrugs)

They got me angry.

REGINA

(ribbing her)

I must never cross you then.

RANI

(smiling)

Yes, even the most famous policewoman in the world had better be careful with me.

REGINA

So you just made up your mind to catch the culprits?

RANI

Yes.

REGINA

You should be on the police force.

RANI

(smiles self-deprecatingly)

Who would hire me?

REGINA

I would. You are one hell of a sleuth.

RANI

They say the pay's no good.

REGINA

You couldn't be making that much more as a yoga teacher.

RANI

Just a little more. I offer fat-cat executives nirvana in seven days. I teach them yoga and meditation at 6 a.m.

REGINA

What a racket! I should pick you up for fraud one of these days.

SCENE 77

Int. Night. In the dining room of the hotel.

Rani and Regina sitting at a table having their last dinner of the holiday. Regina raises a toast.

REGINA

To our last night together. And to Pawan. If he hadn't left we wouldn't have met.

RANI

(not sure if she's quite happy with that toast)

Oh, I hope he has the sense to come back to you.

REGINA

I doubt it. Besides I'm through with him. Thank you for making up that story about your falling out with your boyfriend. *(Rani's face falls. Regina laughs.)* Without your fake suicide attempt, I wouldn't have snapped out of my depression so fast.

RANI

How did you find out?

REGINA

(winks)

Remember, I am a police officer. It's my duty to find out stuff...

SCENE 78

Int. Night. Anzar's apartment.

Anzar listening to a Skype video conversation on his laptop.

MINISTER SANE

(angrily)

Don't call me minister. And no names. Are you sure this techie is not going to blab?

V.O.

I wouldn't worry about him. He's just a whore. He works for whoever pays him top dollar.

MINISTER SANE

I don't want to know anything about him or what you do. All I'm interested in is my percentage.

V.O.

Have I ever let you down?

MINISTER SANE

Not so far. But get rid of him before he gets too big for his boots.

Anzar shuts the laptop, gets up and goes to the mirror.

ANZAR

Just a whore. Whore. *(Pause)* Am I one?

SCENE 79

Anzar is focused on the computer screen on his table. Rani is lying on the bed, reading some costly women's magazine. Rani's unique taste is in evidence everywhere in the flat now. Anzar is a picture of concentration. As is a habit with him, you can hear the sussurus of his whispering as he types away.

RANI

(imitating his pssspssppsss)

Will you stop this psspssspssing. I am reading about life-and-death matters. Should this year's skirts be eight centimetres shorter or fourteen?

ANZAR

My considered opinion is to skip wearing skirts altogether.

RANI

Replace them with what, then? Saris?

ANZAR

How about something pristine? Nothing at all?

RANI

You've got such a dirty mind, Anzar.

ANZAR

(still peering at the screen but mimicking a breathless lover)

That's why you fell madly in love with me.

RANI

(flings the magazine at him)

This is a pure business relationship. I'm hungry as hell. If you don't stop in five minutes, I'm leaving your flat and I'm leaving you for good.

Anzar has seen something on the computer screen which bothers him. He isn't conscious of her any more. He's muttering again but not so softly.

ANZAR

This is the eighth client I've cracked. If I'm the one who broke into the house, obviously I should know how to make it impregnable. I must get to the bottom of this.

RANI

You broke into someone's house?

ANZAR

Yeah, yours. Let's go eat.

SCENE 80

Int. Day. Regina's office.

Regina strides into her office preoccupied and in a hurry. DCP Bilquis Khan is waiting for her.

REGINA

Would you get me the Black Tulip file, please?

DCP KHAN

Hello, remember me? I work here. *(Regina looks puzzled.)*

REGINA

Oh, Bilquis, I'm sorry about my terrible manners but something just occurred to me about that old robbery at the Nandas'.

Bilquis hands over the Nanda robbery file to Regina. Cut to Regina poring over the file and turning pages rapidly. She stops and reads.

REGINA

There. Rani Agarkar. How could I have missed that connection? She was the Nanda's yoga teacher when their safe was cracked. And she was there at the Bank of Baroda robbery.

DCP KHAN

What does that prove?

REGINA

Nothing yet. But let's see.

SCENE 81

Int. Early morning. Regina's apartment.

Regina has an apartment on Nepean Sea Road. From her balcony you can see Priyadarshini Park and beyond it, the Indian Ocean. Regina is taking yoga lessons from Rani. She is trying to do the starting pose of yoga, the padmasan.

REGINA

My limbs are made of petrified wood. I'll never be able to do yoga.

RANI

Just a little practice and you'll be doing fine. Watch.

Rani does the padmasan step-by-step. She's a fine teacher but today is not Regina's day.

REGINA

Why did you follow me to Udaipur?

RANI

You could say I've been stalking you since the time you first appeared in the media. I can quote you in my sleep. I can relate your career case by case. You're my hero.

SCENE 82

Int. Day. Rani's flat.

Rani is busy writing a note when the ink in her ballpen runs out. She tries to open a drawer of the table while going over what she's written when her hand touches the bottom of the drawer. Her face registers surprise. She does a thorough search of the apartment and pulls out

something from underneath the drawer. It's a tiny microphone. Rani dismantles the phone next to her bed and spots a surveillance mike placed in it. She lets it sit there and goes over the rest of her house and discovers a mike in the shade covering the ceiling light in her bedroom. Once again she does not remove the mike.

RANI

She's on to me. *(Smiles as if she is itching for a fight.)* The game's just hotting up.

SCENE 83

Ext. Night. Outside the Siddhi Vinayak temple.

Anzar and Firodia are standing in a very long queue outside the temple in the early hours of Tuesday morning.

ANZAR

What's up?

FIRODIA

There's a super-urgent job that has to be delivered almost overnight.

ANZAR

I told you I am going on leave. Besides, I already have three assignments on my plate.

FIRODIA

Put them aside for a few days.

ANZAR

I've been working non-stop. I'm taking a holiday.

FIRODIA

(shakes his head)

I will pay you twice your normal fee.

ANZAR

I'm sorry. What's the rush, anyway?

FIRODIA

You name the price, no questions asked.

ANZAR

Thank you, but I've already booked tickets to Paris.

FIRODIA

What if I told you, this time you not only crack the code, you also build the new firewall?

ANZAR

(surprised)

You're not serious.

FIRODIA

Yes, I am.

SCENE 84

Int. Night. Rani's bedroom.

A Regina scrapbook is open on the bed. Rani puts the fake Ranjeet Singh jewellery at the bottom of her capacious Gucci bag. Then she unfolds an expensive man's silk kerchief. It's off-white and has a thin red border. She places some very expensive cosmetics, perfume, comb, shades, hair brush and a Cartier pen in the kerchief and places it above the fake jewellery and then tops it with her scarf. Now, she practises pulling out the scarf so that the cosmetics and other items fall out.

SCENE 85

Int. Day. Rani's apartment.

Rani's phone rings a few times before she picks it up.

RANI

Hello, Mrs Drego. How are you?

Cut to the surveillance room at the police headquarters with officers listening to various tapped phones. You hear Rani's voice on one of the lines.

RANI

(off-screen)

I'm really sorry, I can't make it tomorrow. I've an appointment with Mewar Jewellers at 3. How about the day after?

Cut back to Rani's place.

RANI

I'll be there. Bye, now.

SCENE 86

Int. Late night. Anzar's apartment.

ANZAR

(concentrating and talking to himself)

The 'whore' wants to know why the sudden change of heart, Mr Firodia? I promise you I will get to the bottom of this mystery.

SCENE 87

Int./Ext. Day. Rani's apartment.

Rani picks up her bag and car key and makes for the door. Cut to outside Rani's apartment. Rani closes the door and sticks a thin two-inch transparent sticking tape in such a way that part of it is on the top of the doorframe and part on the door.

SCENE 88

Ext. Day. Building opposite Mewar Jewellers.

Rani is on the terrace of a building. She has binoculars in her hands and is watching the street and the pavements. A taxi drives up to the pavement opposite Mewar Jewellers. DCP Khurana and DCP Khan, dressed in the sari-uniform that saleswomen from Mewar Jewellers wear, emerge from it and walk into the store. Regina gets off from the front seat, pays off the cab and takes her position inside Ishwardas

Jewellers in the building opposite the one Rani is in. Rani looks at her watch.

RANI

(to herself)

Two o'clock. I'll be back within half an hour.

SCENE 89

Ext. Day. Outside the House of Rare Jewels.

A Mercedes drives past Mewar Jewellers and comes to a stop in a lane next to the rear entrance to The House of Rare Jewels. Rani steps out in a severe Armani bottle-green, knee-length dress with a bottle-green jacket of the same material. She's wearing a dark-green hat with lace covering part of her face. She's also wearing very large, expensive shades. The effect is one of elegance and aristocratic breeding and bearing. Ghanshyambhai rushes out to greet and accompany her. She smiles shyly.

GHANSHYAMBHAI

Greetings, Miss Elena Chirac. And congratulations on your engagement to Raffael Dumont. It's an honour to welcome the greatest French actress of her generation in our humble shop.

RANI

(in a mild French accent)

I thought my secretary warned you not to use my name or mention my engagement to Raffael.

GHANSHYAMBHAI

She did. She even told me you hated the press and were coming incognito. But I couldn't resist congratulating you. My lips are sealed from now onwards.

RANI

(blushes and responds in a soft voice)

Thank you.

SCENE 90

Int. Day. Exclusive VIP room above on the mezzanine floor in the House of Rare Jewels.

It's a large room with three counters, full-length mirrors and private but open areas for consultations. Three people from Alexander and Rutherford Art Auctioneers, two men and a woman, are already seated in one of the private areas. Ghanshyambhai's younger brother Narottambhai is taking care of them. There's one of those proverbial silences when Rani enters. Ghanshyambhai escorts Rani to a private corner. Cut to camera on the ceiling. Rani makes sure that the camera can see only her veiled profile.

GHANSHYAMBHAI

What will you have, ma'am? Tea, coffee?

RANI

Nothing, thank you.

GHANSHYAMBHAI

You can't come to our place and not have anything.

Indian sweets and tea are served. Ghanshyambhai selects a heavy necklace studded with big precious stones and hands it to Rani. Rani looks at it and flinches just a shade. No one but Ghanshyambhai is aware of this. She puts it around her neck.

GHANSHYAMBHAI

This is the piece, *(softly)* the one from the Jaipur maharani's collection, that your fiancé's mother wanted me to show you.

RANI

Thank you.

Rani looks at herself in the mirror. Its value is undeniable but it does not really go with Rani's personality. Rani is demurely eating the sweets.

GHANSHYAMBHAI

Forgive the presumption, but may I show you a few other pieces?

Rani is noncommital. Ghanshyambhai offers Rani a necklace and earrings with diamonds. Rani tries the necklace and earrings hesitantly. Ghanshyambhai produces three more sets in sapphires, topaz, Basra pearls and one in varied stones. Rani tries them all. The Alexander and Rutherford Art people across are watching.

RANI

Thank you so much. I must go now. Please bring them over tomorrow to the Jewel in the Crown suite and Raf's mother will decide.

GHANSHYAMBHAI

Yes, we'll look forward to that.

He closes the boxes, then dips into the safe and brings out another box.

RANI

No more, please.

GHANSHYAMBHAI

One last piece.

He has opened the box. Sitting in it on a bed of white silk is the legendary Ranjeet Singh set of emeralds of staggering beauty. It is obvious that Ghanshyambhai is not only a fine salesman but also has an understanding of the chemistry between a piece of jewellery and the person who wears it. Rani stares at the necklace in muted but visible amazement. Not a word is spoken. Slowly, after a long pause, she picks it up and wears it and then puts on the earrings. She turns her neck slowly towards the mirror and looks at her reflection. It is only then that Ghanshyambhai, Narottambhai and the Alexander and Rutherford people who have watched as if they were frozen, seem to heave a collective sigh of admiration. Rani looks truly stunning. Again no flashiness. But however subdued, she's a show-stopper.

GHANSHYAMBHAI

Ranjeet Singh ordered that necklace and the rest of the set for his wife but unfortunately, by the time it was ready, she had passed away.

Rani opens her bag, takes out her cell phone and, as if on automatic, dials a number.

RANI

Geraldine, it's me, Elena. *(Pause)* Yes, it's lovely, but a trifle heavy. *(Pause)* Ghanshyambhai showed me an emerald set Ranjeet Singhji had got made for his wife. It does look rather good. *(Pause)* No, of course the final choice is yours. *(Her face crumbles.)* Of course, I'll wear what you choose for me for the wedding.

Even as she speaks, Rani has already taken off the necklace and the earrings. You can see that she's holding back her tears. Everybody tries to look away politely. She too looks away as her hand moves towards her handbag. She unzips her bag agitatedly to remove her kerchief. But as she picks up the scarf to get at it, a whole lot of cosmetics, shades and hairbrush etc., tumble out. She bends down but Ghanshyambhai and even two of the Alexander and Rutherford people are helping to pick them up. Rani now puts the necklace and earrings back in their box and smiles tentatively at everybody.

RANI

You've been patient with me. Thank you. *(Her voice falters almost imperceptibly.)* I'm afraid I got carried away. My mother-in-law, Geraldine, studied jewellery design in Paris and is a far better judge than I. When you come over to the suite, you can show her whatever you like.

Fiona Hartford, the woman from Alexander and Rutherford's, quietly makes her way to Rani.

FIONA

Would you take offence if I introduced myself?

Rani shakes her head ever so slowly.

FIONA

(almost apologetically)

My name's Fiona Hartford. My colleagues and I are from Alexander and Rutherford Art Auctioneers.

RANI

Delighted to meet you.

FIONA

I don't mean to be rude to your mother-in-law. But take the emerald set. I've never seen anyone look so beautiful.

RANI

(stares at her, then speaks)

That is kind of you. *(Pause)* But it's her wedding present to me. I have no say in the matter.

GHANSHYAMBHAI

May I make a suggestion? Take the emerald set with you. If your mother-in-law doesn't approve of it, we'll take it back. But she might just change her mind if she sees it on you.

RANI

(her delicate fingers linger over the emerald necklace one last time, longingly)

I know you mean well but but she has very strong views.

FIONA

In that case, would you mind it very much if we looked at it?

RANI

(smiles for the first time)

But, of course, not. I must take your leave now.

SCENE 91

Int. Night. Anzar's room.

ANZAR

(at his desktop)

Okay Mr Firodia, the midwife has delivered your emergency baby. Now if instead of your 'whore', you yourself are up to dirty tricks, let me buy some emergency insurance. *(Puts in a tracer.)* First a

tracer to follow the new firewall's journey and then I'll just add a rare spice called the disabling function.

SCENE 92

Int. Early morning. Regina's office.

The Alexander and Rutherford Art Auctioneers team is sitting in Regina's office.

REGINA

Let me understand this. You bought the Ranjeet Singh jewels knowing fully well that they cannot be taken out of the country and now you wish to file a case that the House of Rare Jewels cheated you?

FIONA HARTFORD

Yes.

REGINA

You've obviously not seen today's headlines.

She pushes the newspaper she's been reading towards the Alexander and Rutherford team. The headline reads: 'Black Tulip strikes again. Saves national treasure.' 'Black Tulip rescues Ranjeet Singh jewels. Couriers them to Governor.'

FIONA HARTFORD

(reads)

'What belongs to India must stay in India.'

REGINA

You are welcome to file a case. But the authorities may slap a suit against you.

Cut to the Alexander and Rutherford people leaving as DCP Khan walks into Regina's office. Cut to Regina looking at the coloured picture of the Ranjeet Singh jewels on the front page of a daily. She smiles, half in admiration, half bitterly.

REGINA

Touché, Black Tulip. Very smart.

DCP KHAN

(at Regina's table)

We were just a few shops away. How did we not catch her?

REGINA

Because she made sure that we were in the wrong shop. Her research is meticulous and she plans her every move to the last detail. She doesn't go for hi-tech. She keeps it simple, very simple. And she makes constant eye-contact with the owners but at the same time makes sure the camera never catches her face.

DCP KHAN

What are we waiting for? Let's pick her up.

REGINA

On what grounds?

DCP KHAN

We know she did it.

REGINA

No judge is going to buy that. She ensured the jewels didn't leave the country. Plus, she sent them to the governor for safekeeping. *(Pause)* Black Tulip is already a kind of a Robin Hood. Take her in now and we'll turn her into a living legend.

DCP KHAN

So we let her go?

REGINA

She's going to strike again soon.

DCP KHAN

How would you know?

REGINA

She likes money but she likes the excitement even more. Make a list of big-time jewellers. And another of anonymous jewellers, legal and illegal, who deal in heirlooms worth at least five crore per item. We'll keep a watch on them and ask permission to tap their phones. Her research will be her undoing.

SCENE 93

Int. Past midnight. Office of the Director-General of Police.

Director-General of Police Goray walking very briskly into his office. There are four others including Regina Fielding of the rank of commissioners and additional commissioners of police already waiting outside his office. They all salute DGP Goray as he walks into his room and dials a number on a red phone marked 'Hotline'. The clock on the wall shows 3 am.

DGP GORAY

Hello, Ralph. Something must be really wrong for you to ask me to call you at this hour and that too, on the hotline.

V.O.

Hello, Deepak. I wanted absolute privacy.
Hence the call at this unearthly hour.

DGP GORAY

I'm listening with four of my closest associates, all of them commissioners of police.

V.O.

Interpol has learnt that a massive attack on your city is imminent.
The problem is while our sources are reliable,
the information is vague.

DGP GORAY

I'm still listening.

V.O.

The Indian Mujahideen haven't had a really spectacular success in all these years. They want to be taken seriously by the Indian government as well as by the ISI in Pakistan and al-Qaeda and the Taliban.

DGP GORAY

Do we have any hard information?

V.O.

Yes. I quote: '9/11 will look like child's play. We will give Mumbai a shock the likes of which they have never experienced before.' End of quote.

DGP GORAY

Are we talking about a nuclear attack?

V.O.

Your guess is as good as mine. I'll call you if we get any specific information. Bye.

DGP GORAY

Thank you. Bye. *(Addressing the others in the room.)* Well. We now know something and yet know nothing. One thing is certain—this is the big one. Activate all our sources. Cancel all leave applications.

REGINA

Will you ask the High Court's permission to hack the email accounts of all the suspects?

DGP GORAY

Good idea. I will also talk to the chief minister. I take it you know this is absolutely top secret.

CP GHOSH

What shall we name the operation?

DGP GORAY

Operation Agatha. No preconceptions. Follow every lead and trust your gut instincts. We meet every morning.

SCENE 94

Ext. Day. An abandoned tar road in the countryside.

Rani and Anzar are on cycles. Rani is singing 'Hum dono, do premee duniya chhod chale'. *She stops singing suddenly in the middle of the song.*

RANI

Come on, I'll race you.

ANZAR

(emits a fake laugh with a macho swagger)

A bit of realism, madam, might not be out of place.

RANI

Come on.

ANZAR

Don't cry afterwards, 'Ma, Anzar beat me.'

RANI

You've got a hope

She takes off. He follows at top speed. Both are peddling like mad but Rani shoots forward. Four hundred metres later she notices that she's alone. She looks around, Anzar is nowhere to be seen. She pedals back frantically. Anzar is sitting in the grass lost in thought, his chin propped on his wrist. Rani stops her bike and calls out.

RANI

I thought you said you were going to beat me?

ANZAR

(absent-mindedly)

I think he's taken me for a ride.

RANI

Who?

ANZAR

(shrugs his shoulders)

Just talking about work.

RANI

Do you have any idea what a scare you gave me disappearing from the scene?

ANZAR

(still to himself, abruptly)

I've to go back home.

RANI

We're supposed to spend the day together. You promised.

ANZAR

I'm sorry. It's important.

RANI

What's wrong, Anzar?

ANZAR

I have to check something.

RANI

Can't it wait? *(Pause)* You want to break up with me?

ANZAR

(completely taken aback, brusque)

No. *(Pause)* No.

He goes off. She shakes her head as if she doesn't believe him.

SCENE 95

Ext. Day. The terrace of an old five-storeyed building.

DCP SHARMA

The last two tips you gave were a dead loss. Why should I believe you this time?

CHHOTA PEG

Life's a game of dice, Sharma Sahab. You win some, you lose some.

DCP SHARMA

(in mock surprise)

Wow. What we've got here is a philosopher.

CHHOTA PEG

You don't have to buy my story, Sahab. Just don't complain afterwards I didn't warn you.

REGINA

(listening to the conversation from her car parked down the road)

Ask him how much plastic?

DCP SHARMA

How many boatloads of plastic explosives were offloaded and where?

CHHOTA PEG

I won't swear this on the Holy Book but I heard seven dhows.

Sharma catches him by the throat and presses his Adam's apple.

DCP SHARMA

You expect me to believe that cock-and-bull story? Seven dhows in the Mumbai monsoons?

Chhota Peg screams and then the screams are stifled.

REGINA

Let him go, Sharma.

CHHOTA PEG

(utterly out of breath)

I take all the risks and give you the dope and in exchange you throttle me. This must be Ramrajya, a just world.
And the best of worlds.

SCENE 96

Int. Noon. Regina's office

All the senior staff are standing while Regina is drawing circles on a roughly drawn map of Mumbai with the name of each ACP allotted to a particular circle.

REGINA

A huge amount of RDX has arrived by sea. You now know which area you are responsible for. Get cracking. Check with every source you can. Get your informants to talk. Come back with results. The fate of the city depends on you.

SCENE 97

Int. Night. Anzar's apartment.

Anzar is clicking away madly at his desktop and then stares flabbergasted at what he sees.

ANZAR

Oh my God, what a fool I've been. I bought that line about designing failsafe firewalls along with the client. My arse, all you wanted, Firodia, was to sell the secrets of the Fortune 500 companies to the highest bidder.

SCENE 98

Ext. Past midnight. Rani's building.

A car drops Rani at her buiding. Anzar is sitting at the entrance of the building in a midnight-blue shirt. There are black circles around his eyes. He looks haggard as if he has not eaten or slept for days. After a fairly long goodbye, the car door closes and Rani walks into her building to find Anzar waiting for her. Throughout the earlier part of the conversation she pointedly refuses to look at him.

ANZAR

Long time to get back home and an even longer goodbye.

RANI

(smiles sweetly)

You're not the only game in town. Besides, I don't like being with someone who suffers from an attention deficit syndrome.

She walks up to the lift.

ANZAR

I've been waiting for over four hours.

RANI

Just four hours? I've waited for days.

ANZAR

May I come up with you?

RANI

What for?

ANZAR

This is going to sound phoney but I have had some kind of ethical crisis.

RANI

Sure, the fate and future of the country rest on your shoulders.

ANZAR

I've behaved abominably. I'm sorry, I really am. *(No response from Rani.)* I'll see you. *(He turns around and leaves.)*

RANI

Where the hell do you think you're going? *(She looks at him for the first time.)* What have you gone and done to yourself? When was the last time you ate? Or slept?

ANZAR

I don't remember. The food in the fridge got over and then I got caught up with work.

RANI

First, I'm going to feed you till you're bursting at the seams. And then as soon as I complete my next three-day scam yoga workshop for MDs and CEOs, we are going on a holiday.

ANZAR

Who's paying?

RANI

Who else? You.

Cut to …

SCENE 99

Int. Morning. Rani's bedroom.

They're lying a littled cramped in the bed. Anzar is in his favourite T-shirt, the one with an adorable dog. Rani gets out of bed while Anzar tries to stop her.

RANI

You hog the whole bed. Next time you sleep on the floor or buy me a super-king-sized bed. No, buy me a three-bedroom apartment. *(Goes to the door and picks up two newspapers and glances at them.)* Hey, look at this. *(Throws the papers on the bed.)*

ANZAR

What's it?

RANI

(reads from the first paper)

The 's' 'h' asterix asterix hits the fan. Hacker 'Conscience' blows the lid off Minister-mafia-private enterprise nexus. Here's the second headline: Whistle blower 'Conscience' reveals Minister Sane for sale to highest bidder.

ANZAR

(shrugs)

What's the big deal? This is India. You can buy anybody. Who knows, maybe you and me too.

RANI

(sounding superior)

Certainly not the Additional Commissioner of Police, Regina Fielding.

SCENE 100

Ext. Day. Minister Sane's lawns.

A press conference is in progress.

MINISTER SANE

Would I be sitting here if I was guilty? My conscience is clear. And so is my record.

FIRST JOURNALIST

Are you saying the detailed figures in the papers and on the Net are fabrications?

MINISTER SANE

It's quite simple. It's a conspiracy. There is a foreign hand at work here.

SECOND JOURNALIST

That excuse is old hat, Minister. What are you going to do about it?

MINISTER

I intend to wipe out crime from this city. It won't be able to breathe in my state.

FIRST JOURNALIST

But the chief minister says he's going to set up a commission to investigate the charges against you.

MINISTER SANE

That he must if I'm to be proven completely innocent. But remember truth will triumph. Satyameva jayate.

SCENE 101

Int. Morning. Rani's apartment.

Rani's latest designer suitcase is packed. She's dressed in travelling clothes and is applying lipstick while talking to Anzar on her cell phone.

RANI

Are you packed?

ANZAR

All set to go.

RANI

Passport?

ANZAR

Yee-es.

RANI

Toothbrush? I will not allow you to use mine.

ANZAR

Yeee-es. I've taken seven of them, one for each day.

RANI

Seven pairs of socks?

ANZAR

Yeee-es. Every single sock is of a different colour.

RANI

Swimming trunks?

ANZAR

Yeeeee-es, Maman. The one with 'Ready for action' printed on the crotch.

RANI

(ignores his ribald comments)

Some decent clothes?

ANZAR

Yeeeeee-es, Maman. I'm wearing the shiny pink polyester suit with a parrot-green waistcoat.

RANI

I'm on my way. Be there in twenty minutes.

Cut to Rani picking up the morning papers at her door and taking the lift down. Cut to Rani in the cab as it goes toward Bandra. She's looking at the headlines. '"Conscience" does it again. Everybody who's anybody is on the take'. 'The mafia gives, Minister Sane takes'. 'Politicos panic as "Conscience" lets the cat out of the bag'.

Cut to …

SCENE 102

Int. Morning. Landing of Anzar's flat.

Rani is banging the door to Anzar's flat.

RANI

Open the bloody door, Anzar. This is no time to play the fool. Where the hell are you? I'll never never never talk to you again if you don't turn up the next minute.

She knocks on a neighbour's door. Mrs Dixit opens it.

RANI

Sorry to bother you this early but Anzar and I were going on a week's holiday.

MRS DIXIT

I know. He told me to take care of his place.

RANI

I called him up just before leaving. But now he's not responding. He had told me you have a set of spare keys.

Mrs Dixit rings the bell to Anzar's flat. Total silence. She goes into her flat, gets the spare keys and opens Anzar's apartment. Rani rushes in. Anzar's suitcase is packed and ready next to the door. Rani goes into the rest of the apartment. There's no sign of Anzar.

RANI

His computer's missing. Where could he have gone? Thank you, Mrs Dixit. I'll wait half an hour for him and then leave.

Cut to Rani back in a taxi. She looks lost and very down.

SCENE 103

Int. Day. Conference room in the minister's office.

All the top brass in the police department, including Regina, are present while the minister holds a briefing.

MINISTER SANE

Let me not beat about the bush. Lazy times are over. You are going to pick up every single small, big and medium-sized criminal in the city.

DCP KHAN

Where are we going to accommodate them?

MINISTER SANE

In the jails. Let's hope the majority will end up dead for lack of air.

DGP GORAY

Such indiscriminate action may lead to a serious backlash.

MINISTER SANE

Are you afraid to do your duty, DGP Goray? *(There is a shocked silence.)* I take it then that the briefing is over.

REGINA

What about the criminal element amongst the politicians?

MINISTER SANE

What about them?

REGINA

Do we pick them up too?

MINISTER

What do you think, ACP Fielding?

REGINA

I don't think, Minister. I merely follow orders.

MINISTER SANE

There's only one way things are done in Maharashtra. The law is blind to rank or position.

SCENE 104

Int. Night. Rani's bedroom.

RANI

It's one past 12. Where are you, Anzar?

Cut to Rani flicking channels. CNN, BBC, AL JAZEERA. Cut to Rani putting on her yoga clothes.

RANI

Six a.m. If you are not here before I come back from Regina's place, I'm through with you, Anzar.

Cut to Rani getting out of the yoga clothes. She talks on her cellphone.

RANI

Pick up the phone, Anzar. Pickuppickuppickuppickup. I'm warning you, Anzar. Don't try my patience. That's it. Divorce. There's no going back even if you beg me on your knees.

SCENE 105

Int. Day. Lift.

Lily Pinto and Rani going up in the lift.

LILY

Where are we going?

RANI

I haven't slept two nights. Let's go take a massage at the Born Again parlour. It's on me.

LILY

You're the mistress of yoga and you can't sleep? *(Lily's cellphone rings. She looks at the number and grimaces.)* It's my day off. *(She answers the phone, listens intently and frowns.)* I'll be there within half an hour. *(Disconnects)* May I take a rain check on the massage?

RANI

What's the matter?

LILY

(preoccupied and worried)

Conscience has gone missing.

RANI

You mean the one who's outed all the scams? *(Lily nods her head.)* I'll drop you at the office. *(Smiles wryly.)* Maybe Conscience is just taking a break.

LILY

(shakes her head)

If his cover's blown, all the folks he has exposed will want him dead.

SCENE 106

Int. Night. Rani's flat.

Rani has dark circles around her eyes and looks utterly worn out as she switches on her laptop.

RANI

Come back, Anzar. Are you okay? Where are you? Wonder what Regina's up to. *(She scrolls through Regina's messages.)* Top priority. Top secret. To select computer personnel. 'I want every single senior executive of the multinationals "Conscience" blew the whistle on, tailed. Find "Conscience". Alive, not dead.' Email from 'Conscience'. *(Reads)* S. O. What's S.O.? Son of a bitch? What's the date? Three days ago? And the time? That's the time I left home to pick Anzar up. S.O.S. Oh my god. It's Anzar and his ethical dilemma. Oh no, it can't be. Oh you stupid fool.

SCENE 107

Int. Early morning. Rani's apartment.

Rani calls Lily on her cell phone.

RANI

Hi, Lily. Care for a bite?

LILY

A hundred bites would be better. And a shower and a twenty four-hour nap. But I can't. I'm on the job.

RANI

What if I get your breakfast over in the car?

LILY

I can't possibly ask you to deliver breakfast.

RANI

The eggs and croissants are getting cold. Yes or no?

Cut to…

SCENE 108

Int. Early morning. Police headquarters.

Lily sitting in the car just outside the police headquarters opposite Crawford Market.

LILY

Now I know what ambrosia is. You're an angel, Rani Agarkar.

RANI

So was Satan.

LILY

(biting into a croissant)

That woman is a slave driver except she drives herself the hardest.

RANI

Who?

LILY

Who else? ACP Regina Fielding. They're out for her blood.

RANI

Why? She's the best cop in the country. And honest, to boot.

LILY

(smiles wryly)

What better reason than that? If they could, they would bump her off.

RANI

I would have thought the first on the list is 'Conscience'.

LILY

He is. His only hope is Regina Fielding.

A man on a cycle wearing a uniform labelled 'Urgent Couriers' appears at the gate of the police headquarters.

COURIER BOY

Do you know where I can find Laila Pinto.

LILY

Lily Pinto, not Laila Pinto.

COURIER BOY

Laila or Lily, so long as the address is correct. Please sign.

Lily signs and opens the packet. Courier leaves. There's a note and an unmistakable red T-shirt with a fluffy dog that the audience will have seen Anzar wearing in Rani's bedroom.

LILY

(reading the note)

Dear Inspector Lily, get your three police dogs to smell the T-shirt and take them to the locations where 'Conscience' was consulting. You'll find 'Conscience' within the next few hours. Time's running out.

LILY

(laughing)

What do you make of that, Rani?

RANI

(shrugs)

Looks like a crank letter. But what do you have to lose?

SCENE 109

Int. Evening. Rani's apartment.

RANI

(on the phone)

Any luck? Did that T-shirt lead you anywhere?

LILY

We thought we had found 'Conscience' when our ace dog barked near the dicky of Samrat Firodia's BMW. We got it opened but the dog had obviously made a mistake.

RANI

Did you talk to Firodia?

LILY

He had just got back from Calcutta and showed us his boarding passes.

RANI

What about the BMW?

LILY

In the garage for repairs. We checked. It had been there for the three days Firodia was out of town.

RANI

What now?

LILY

It doesn't look good.

SCENE 110

Int. Night. Rani's apartment.

RANI

(talking to herself)

Who gives a damn about your conscience or your ethical crisis, Anzar? Talk to me. What should I do? I hate you. You're going to destroy everything I've worked for. Why should I give a damn about what happens to you? You got what you wanted, you became an overnight hero. Except you might already be a dead hero.

SCENE 111

Int. Night. Outside Regina's apartment.

Rani's finger is pressed on the bell of Regina's flat. The door opens abruptly. Regina is getting into her uniform.

REGINA

What the … .What are you doing here at this hour?

RANI

I wanted to talk to you.

REGINA

Bad timing. I'm busy.

RANI

It's about 'Conscience'.

REGINA

(looks around to see if anybody's listening)

Come in. Talk. I'm running against time.

RANI

My friend Anzar has been missing for three days.

REGINA

So? Go to the missing persons' bureau ... Your boyfriend?

RANI

He's a computer whiz and I suspect was working for Firodia. I'm almost certain he's Conscience.

REGINA

Why should I believe you? How do I know you are not one of Firodia's moles? The last time I trusted you, you played me for a sucker.

RANI

(looks hurt)

I just wanted to get to know you. I've hero-worshipped you since I don't remember when.

REGINA

Tell me another. You were snooping on me to find out police secrets.

RANI

(silent for a bit)

I sent the T-shirt that Conscience wore at my place to Lily.

REGINA

Yes? That T-shirt didn't lead to anything.

RANI

I know.

The phone rings and Regina picks it up. She listens for a minute and then speaks on the phone.

REGINA

Stay right there and report any new developments to me. *(Speaks to Rani)* Firodia's just left his home. I'm going to track him.

RANI

If the T-shirt was a false clue, why are you still following him?

REGINA

The boot of the BMW had been newly painted from inside. Maybe that's why the dog got confused.

RANI

From inside? Isn't that a little odd?

REGINA

Yes.

She pushes Rani out of the door and follows her after closing the door shut.

RANI

May I come with you?

Cut to the two of them in the lift. Regina looks at Rani quizzically.

REGINA

It's a police job. You have a better policewoman's nose than the real ones. Get in.

RANI

Thank you.

REGINA

Do you have any idea what the consequences of your coming to me are going to be?

RANI

I have.

REGINA

I doubt it. You'll have to confess every crime you committed, Black Tulip. Don't forget our jails are hell on earth.

RANI

I want Anzar back. Alive.

REGINA

You don't have to worry about Conscience. I'll do my best to get him back alive. It's my job.

RANI

I'm coming with you.

REGINA

(reading an SMS on her cell phone as they get into her car)

Firodia's got on to the Chavan Mumbai–Pune Expressway.

SCENE 112

Ext. Night. The Chavan Mumbai-Pune Expressway.

Regina places the police siren on the car roof. Cut to the police car speeding madly. Cut to the car on the expressway. Regina switches off the siren, her hand reaches out to the top of the car, removes the siren and puts it beside her. Soon, they are tailing Firodia's car.

REGINA

You were making enough as a yoga teacher. Why risk everything?

RANI

I swore I wouldn't be anyone's slave again. Anybody who is making big money is playing the market or is in IT. I had zero interest in IT and no aptitude for the market. Since I wanted to be super rich in a hurry, I didn't have too many choices.

REGINA

What kind of game were you playing with me? It was not a simple cat-and-mouse situation.

RANI

(smiles)

You were the best. I didn't want anyone to get the better of you … except me.

Cut to Firodia on the Mumbai–Pune Expressway followed at a measured distance by Regina. There's a thick mist. Cut to the Khandala ghats and on to Lonavla. The BMW suddenly swerves to the right and crosses the railway line, turns right again and after a short while turns into a broad private road lined with old spacious bungalows with large compounds full of huge trees that conceal the houses on both sides. Regina slows down and follows Firodia far more circumspectly. She loses him and finds herself at the end of the road. From this point, the woods start. She turns left when she realizes that Firodia has turned into the corner house, with 'Samrat' written on its gate, and parked the car almost halfway inside the compound in front of the house.

REGINA

You stay put. If Firodia's armed, my priority's to grab him. You take care of Anzar.

Regina gets out of the car and closes the door softly. Firodia jumps out of his car with a laptop bag. Cut to a close-up of the bag which has Anzar's name emblazoned on it. Instead of entering the ancient but well-kept bungalow through the front doors, he moves to the left and unlocks a side door that leads to a cellar full of furniture, vessels, files and other junk and closes the door behind him. Regina follows him and strains her ears to hear what is going on in the cellar.

Cut to cellar wth a dim light. Anzar is lying in a heap on the floor, his hands and feet tied.

SCENE 113

Int./Ext. Night. Cellar/Compound outside cellar.

ANZAR

(croaks)

Water. Please, water.

FIRODIA

(kicks him in the chest)

You little shit. I give you a job, pay you a fancy fee and you bite the hand that feeds you. How does it feel, going without water for three days?

ANZAR

Water. Please.

Firodia kicks him again. Talks as he bends down and unties Anzar's hands.

FIRODIA

You'll get water after you pull out all the dirt on Minister Sane. Here's your laptop. I can then do some reverse blackmailing to save my own arse.

Firodia hoists Anzar up roughly and seats him on the chair. What transpires now is like a Punch and Judy show. Every time Anzar is propped up, he keels over. Firodia hits him again and roughly lifts him up and makes him sit. The next minute, Anzar is again down on the floor. Firodia places the laptop on the table after attaching the wi-fi dongle.

FIRODIA

Get down to work, you asshole. I'm not buying that fake fainting.

Firodia's rant has no effect on Anzar. The guy hasn't had water or food for days and is incapable of sitting up.

ANZAR

Water.

Firodia's backhand flashes past and hits Anzar in the face. Anzar's lip is torn and bleeding and he's lying inert on the floor. Firodia shakes him by the shoulders when it dawns on him that the man has passed out. He kicks Anzar hard in the chest and ferrets out an old, dusty glass jug. In the process a whole load of stuff comes tumbling down, making a lot of noise. Firodia impatiently rushes past Anzar. He's almost at the door. Throughout the entire sequence, the camera will cut to Regina listening at the door and Rani watching the scene surreptitiously through the intense mist.

REGINA

(whispers to herself)

I failed you, Bijlee. Don't let me fail again, please.

The door opens so suddenly, Regina is thrown to the floor on her back and the jug falls on her but doesn't break. Firodia is as surprised as her.

FIRODIA

What the fuck!

Firodia runs like crazy to the back of his BMW, flings open the door and pulls out the gun lying on the seat. Regina's already up, has pulled her gun out of the holster and runs to the corner of the building.

REGINA

Drop the gun or I'll shoot.

But Firodia has already fired at her. Regina pulls away but the bullet hits the wall and ricochets to lodge in her right arm. Regina steadies her right hand by gripping it with her left. Firodia is inside the car and reverses it, making a frightful screeching noise. She shoots one tyre and then the next. The BMW swerves crazily. Cut to Rani opening her handbag, taking out her sling, bending down to pick up a round pebble-like stone. Cut to Firodia jumping out and beginning to run towards the woods, turning every now and then to fire at Regina. Cut to Rani pulling the rubber straps of the sling taut and letting go. The stone hits Firodia dead centre of the forehead. He sways and crumples to the ground. Regina gets up painfully and is walking towards Firodia when he gets up and aims at Regina.

REGINA

Freeze. Or I'll shoot.

Firodia fires. And so does Regina as she jumps away. This time Firodia does not get up. Regina now has a bullet lodged in her thigh and sits down.

In the meantime, Rani has entered the compound and made her way to the cellar. She sees Anzar lying on the floor.

ANZAR

Water, please.

Rani picks up the jug lying at the door, goes to the tap which supplies water to the garden, washes it clean, fills it up and brings it over to Anzar. He nearly drops it. She holds it to his mouth. Then she picks him up and the laptop, carries him to Regina's car. She goes to Regina, helps her into the seat next to the driver's.

REGINA

You think you can carry Firodia too?

RANI

A lifetime of yoga. I'll carry two of him.

REGINA

Too bad he's no more. Though I'm sure Minister Sane would have got rid of him in the lock-up before I could have questioned him.

Cut to Rani driving and coming to a halt at a roadside café. She picks up three bottles of mineral water, four packets of glucose biscuits and two cones of ice cream and hands them to Regina and Anzar.

RANI

Where now? A hospital here? Or in Mumbai?

REGINA

Neither. We go to your house first and you get Anzar back on his feet. Bilquis will take me home and get my doctor over.

RANI

And Firodia?

REGINA

Bilquis will take care of him.

RANI

What about me? When do I go into the lock-up?

REGINA

We'll sort that out in a few more days.

SCENE 114

Int. Day. Regina's office.

REGINA

Anzar stays put in your place. No calls, no going out.

RANI

Why?

REGINA

It's the only way to keep him safe. We'll produce a mangled body and leak the story that Firodia killed Conscience but he was himself bumped off, we don't know by whom.

RANI

Anzar is pig-headed but luckily he's in no shape to resist.

REGINA

Sit down. Can I trust you?

RANI

I trusted you even though I knew you would send me to jail.

REGINA

Interpol has warned us of a major terrorist threat to Mumbai. The Indian Mujahideen are going to carry out the attack with the help of the mafia boss Salehbhai.

RANI

What kind of attack?

REGINA

The trouble is we have no idea about the nature of the attack or when and where it will take place.

RANI

My racket was heists, never terror.

REGINA

I know that. But you have contacts with the criminal world. They cleared the expensive goods for you. Don't worry, I don't want their names.

RANI

What do you want from me?

REGINA

Keep your eyes and ears open. I want someone who brings a fresh mindset to the looming crisis in the city.

RANI

Anything else?

REGINA

Yes, why did you follow me to Udaipur and expose Black Tulip?

RANI

This won't make sense. You were my role model but I also wanted to pit myself against you.

SCENE 115

Int. Noon. Abdulbhai's home.

ABDULBHAI

(pushing the plate of fish tikkas towards Rani)

What brings you here today, Rani beti?

RANI

(sighs)

The market's so uneasy. What's going on, Abdulbhai?

ABDULBHAI

I wish I knew.

RANI

Are you expecting trouble?

ABDULBHAI

There's no end to the rumours. My family and I have suffered at the hands of Hindu fundamentalists but if a few stupid jehadis make trouble, thousands from my community will die and rivers of blood will flow.

RANI

Would you be better off in an Islamic country?

ABDULBHAI

(shakes his head and smiles)

This is my country as much as it's yours and that of the Hindu extremists. My son-in-law Farhad believes I am a fool and coward and so does my son who's joined him in Dubai. Sometimes I think we can no longer tell the difference between Allah and Satan. *(Sighs)* Let's hope this madness will pass and pass soon.

SCENE 116

Int. Day. Regina's office.

DGP Goray walks in as Regina gets up to salute him with some effort. DGP signals to her to sit down.

DGP GORAY

Just got a message from Interpol that the attack is imminent.

REGINA

Any clue about which day or date?

DGP GORAY

Nothing precise. Sometime in the next three or four days.

Cut to

SCENE 117

Ext. Day. Bombay Stock Exchange Building / Air India Building / Wankhede Stadium

Regina and DCP Sharma get out of a police jeep. Camera does a tilt-up to take in the BSE building. It seems to go on forever. Cut to basement. Regina and DCP Sharma search the basement, pillar by pillar.

Cut to the Air India building where an all-male police team is checking out the basement and other areas with a team of dogs looking for explosives.

Cut to Wankhede Stadium. Workers are preparing the ground, watering it, running rollers on the pitch. Some are at the high scoreboard, fixing the words 'India versus England'.

Regina, DCP Khan, DCP Sharma and thirty policemen are under the stands, going over the girders, beams and columns.

REGINA

What time is the match?

DCP KHAN

Two o'clock tomorrow.

REGINA

(surprised)

Two o'clock?

DCP SHARMA

It's a day-and-night fixture. There's nothing here. Let's go.

SCENE 118

Int. Night. Rani's apartment.

RANI

(on the phone)

What do you mean he's no more? I was with him this afternoon.

Cut to Rani in Abdulbhai's home which is filled with relatives and friends. Jehan hugs Rani tightly and takes her into her bedroom.

RANI

I'm sorry, sweetheart, I'm so sorry. We had such a long talk. He was like a father to me too. What happened?

JEHAN

I was not in the room but Abbajaan and my brother-in-law, Farhadbhai, who's visiting from Dubai, had an argument about something. I have never seen Abbajaan so angry. And then my father left the house abruptly.

She breaks down and Rani hugs her again.

RANI

It's okay, you can tell me some other time.

JEHAN

But I want to talk. Farhadbhai followed him. We thought Abbajaan had gone to the masjid, at least that's what Farhadbhai told us, but when some unidentified car ran over him, it was near the police station. The one witness who saw it said the car deliberately ran him over. I'm so confused.

RANI

Why would anybody want to kill him?

JEHAN

Farhadbhai says the witness was talking nonsense.

RANI

Why would he do that? Did Abdulbhai have any enemies?

JEHAN

You knew Abbajaan. He kept to himself. But when he felt strongly about something, he did not mince words.

RANI

How about his old friends, did they say anything? Any casual remark that struck you as peculiar?

JEHAN

Not that I can remember.

RANI

If you recollect anything, let me know.

SCENE 119

Int. Morning. Basement of the World Trade Centre.

Regina, DCP Sharma, DCP Khan and Inspector Pinto are working in the basement of the World Trade Centre. Suddenly, Regina speaks up.

REGINA

We're going back to the Wankhede Stadium.

DCP SHARMA

We examined every centimetre of the place yesterday.

REGINA

I want to go back.

INSPECTOR PINTO

Another hour-and-a-half and the crowds will be queuing to get in.

Regina is already going up the stairs.

SCENE 120

Ext. Day. Wankhede Stadium.

Regina, Bilqis and Lily are checking out the premises like women possessed. DCP Sharma rushes to Regina.

DCP SHARMA

ACP Fielding, the crowds are screaming to be let in.

Cut to the crowds outside.

REGINA

Ten more minutes.

DCP SHARMA

You've been saying that for the past hour.

REGINA

Please.

Inspector Pinto who has been checking out one of the steel towers that support the bank of lights comes over to Regina.

INSPECTOR PINTO

(softly)

Will you come with me?

Cut to one of the horizontal right-angled beams in the tower where a timer device is quietly ticking away.

Cut to the crowds trying to break through the cordon of police. Cut to a number of policemen scouring and tracing the wires and the plastic explosives.

Cut to the first ball of the match being bowled. Cut to Regina slumping behind the stands in exhaustion and relief.

REGINA

(to Lily)

The RDX circuity seems to have the hallmark of Salehbhai. Have the plastic explosives sent to the lab for analysis. *(To Bilquis Khan and the other DCPs)* Round up each and every one of Salehbhai's men.

SCENE 121

Int. Night. Rani's apartment.

The cellphone rings. Rani rushes into the kitchen and closes the door since Anzar is fast asleep.

RANI

Yes, Jehan.

JEHAN

You said I should call if I remembered anything.

RANI

Tell me.

JEHAN

I remember my brother-in-law, Farhad, telling my father that there were going to be two Diwalis this year, the Hindu one and an Islamic one. He said we will celebrate fireworks in a million homes.

RANI

Where is he?

JEHAN

My brother and he left for the airport.

RANI

They didn't wait for your father's funeral?

JEHAN

They had some urgent business in Dubai but they'll be back the day after tomorrow.

SCENE 122

(From this scene onwards till the resolution of the crisis, the soundtrack and also all outdoor shots will have Diwali fireworks in the background.)

Int. Night. The lift to Regina's apartment.

As Regina limps back to the lift in her buliding after parking the car, Rani joins her at the landing.

REGINA

What are you doing here? Is your guest okay?

RANI

He's all right. You remember Abdulbhai?

REGINA

(puzzled)

Who's that? I've had a rough day and I'm very tired. Oh, Abdulbhai, the old newspaperman who met with a hit-and-run accident?

RANI

Abdulbhai's son-in-law, Farhad, who was here from Dubai claimed it was an accident but an eyewitness said that a car deliberately ran over him. Farhad also said Abdulbhai was going to the mosque but the accident took place not even five metres from the police station which is in the diagonally opposite direction.

SCENE 123

Int. Night. Regina's apartment.

REGINA

Let's go into the kitchen and make coffee.
I need some shock therapy.

RANI

Farhad apparently mentioned something about two Diwalis, the traditional Hindu one and an Islamic one. And that there would be fireworks in a million homes.

Regina fills the kettle, puts it on the gas burner and switches on the gas.

REGINA

Go on.

RANI

If that's right, the old man going to the police station makes sense. The car was stolen from Abdulbhai's neighbour.

REGINA

Fireworks in a million homes? What do you make of that?

RANI

I've been puzzling over that since the time Jehan, his daughter, spoke to me.

Silence. Both of them are lost in thought.

REGINA

Oops, the water's boiling.

Suddenly Rani jumps up and swtitches off the gas range.

REGINA

Mother of God ... it's Mumbai's piped gas supply system. What time is it?

RANI

Nine thirty-five

REGINA

We don't have time to lose!

RANI

I'll call Jehan just in case we can nab Farhad and get some information from him. *(Punches a key on her cell phone)* Hello, Jehan, which flight did Farhadbhai catch?

JEHAN

(off-screen)

The nine seventeen Etihad flight to Dubai.

RANI

(shakes her head, turns to Regina)

No luck. The flight left on time.

REGINA

Check on Flight Track if the Etihad flight has left.

They rush down the stairs. Regina dials a number.

REGINA

Bilquis, alert DGP Goray. Tell him the stadium attack was a decoy. It's the gas supply system they are about to attack. Put all SOS emergency procedures in place. Get TV stations, private radios and All India Radio, plus Facebook and Twitter to announce that there is a leak in the piped gas supply and ask all users to instantly switch off gadgets running on gas till further notice.

Regina switches off the phone. They are in the basement. Regina gives Rani the car keys. Switches on the siren.

REGINA

Drive to Mahanagar Gas at the Bandra-Kurla Complex . *(Dials another number)* Hello. Is that Mr Mahindra Varma, Managing Director of Mahanagar Gas? This is Additional Commissioner of Police Regina Fielding. There's a serious problem in the state gas facility. Please treat this as an emergency. Meet me at your head office at BKC in twenty minutes.

RANI

The Etihad flight's delayed.

REGINA

(keys in a name)

Sharma, Regina Fielding. Call Air Traffic Control. Stop the Etihad flight. Get airport police to take Farhad Fakri, his son and his brother-in-law into custody and bring them to the Mahanagar Gas head office at the Bandra-Kurla Complex. Call me as soon as you've news.

SCENE 124

Int. Night. The Mahanagar Gas Supply Company offices.

Rani and Regina hovering over Mahindra Varma as he opens his desktop and starts typing.

MAHINDRA VARMA

I know you are both tense but please don't hover over me.

Cut to wall clock. It's 9.50.

MAHINDRA VARMA

I'll key in the emergency procedure coordinates and the main gate will come down and the gas supply will be shut instantly.

Regina's phone rings.

V.O.

We've got them. Since the Etihad flight was delayed, they had already boarded the Emirates flight which was in take-off mode.

REGINA

Good. Put your siren on full blast and race to the Mahanagar Gas Office at BKC.

Cut to Mahindra Varma working desperately on the desktop. Cut to wall clock. It's 9.55, then 10.00. Both Regina and Rani look at each other as they get more and more antsy but keep quiet. Then it's 10.05. At 10.15 Regina rises.

MAHINDRA VARMA

(speaks in a shaky voice)

I'm sorry, they've changed the original firewall and replaced it with a new one. It will take two to three weeks to decode and decommission.

REGINA

You're absolutely certain?

MAHINDRA VARMA

Whoever's designed it has deliberately inserted so many false clues, frankly, I'm afraid it will take much longer to decode.

SCENE 125

Interior. Night. Regina's car.

Rani is driving.

REGINA

Drive to Police HQ. I must brief the DGP. He will have to speak with the chief minister and General Gurmeet Singh, the head of the army. Where are you going? I said HQ.

RANI

If anybody can help, Anzar can.

REGINA

You heard Mahindra Varma. He knows his set-up better than anyone else. We need to warn the whole city.

RANI

We're already there. Anzar will tell us in five minutes.

REGINA

You're wasting precious minutes.

SCENE 126

Int. Night. Rani's apartment.

Rani switches on lights. Anzar is fast asleep. She whisks the coverlet and immediately puts it back. Anzar is naked.

RANI

Wake up, Anzar. It's urgent.

ANZAR

Go away.

RANI

Salehbhai and the Indian Mujahideen have changed the firewall of the Mahanagar Gas Supply and are about to start a fire in a million homes. Mumbai will go up in flames in another forty minutes.

ANZAR

What can I do about it? It will take two to three weeks at the minimum to break into the system. *(Goes back to sleep.)*

REGINA

I told you, you're wasting precious time.

RANI

I'm sorry. I thought Anzar could help.

REGINA

Bye. I am off.

(She's at the door)

ANZAR

(suddenly sits up)

Firewall for which company?

RANI

I told you. Mahanagar Gas Supply.

Anzar wakes up with a start, grabs a pair of trousers and a shirt. He picks up his laptop on the run. He's barefoot. Regina and Rani run behind him.

ANZAR

Take me to the Mahanagar Gas Office.

Cut to the Mahanagar Gas Office.

SCENE 127

Int. Night. Mahanagar Gas Supply Office

ANZAR

Will you please make me some coffee, Rani?

RANI

No, it's too risky to light the gas range just now.

ANZAR

Then get me some bitter chocolate. I need a stimulant to wake me up.

Cut to Rani tearing the cover off a Lindt 70 per cent bar and feeding it to Anzar. Cut to Regina, Rani and Mahindra Varma staring intently at the desktop screen. The firewall is no longer functional.

RANI

Hooray. Yippee.

REGINA

(hugs Anzar)

How did you do it?

ANZAR

This was the last job I did for Firodia. It was the first time in all these months that he asked me to not merely break into an established firewall but to design a new one to replace it. I thought something was fishy and inserted a disabling code just in case.

MAHINDRA VARMA

(fiddles with the keys but the main gate for the gas supply system does not close)

The gate's still open.

ANZAR

Can't be. My software was designed to close it unless … unless they've introduced a new manual override.

MAHINDRA VARMA

(busy tracking the problem and arriving at a major tangle of wires at the other end of the room)

Oh no, they've set up one more trap just in case someone tampers with the new firewall.

RANI

Didn't you just say, Anzar, that you had disabled the firewall?

ANZAR

Yes, I did. But whoever's installed my new firewall had the know-how to program an extra counter-measure. *(Examines the jumble of wires and locates a small gadget that's ticking away)* It triggers a simple electrical impulse that activates a timer. Cut the wrong wire and the whole thing will blow up and the gas will be all over the city.

REGINA

(looks at the clock on the wall … it's 11.55)

You mean it's a bomb.

MAHINDRA VARMA

Something like that but we don't know what explosives they're using.

Four minutes and fifty-four seconds to go on the timer. Regina punches a key on her cellphone.

REGINA

Bilquis, please rush our bomb team over to the Mahanagar Gas Supply Office. And alert every fire station in the city about an emergency.

MAHINDRA VARMA

(shaking his head)

Too late.

Enter DCP Sharma with Farhad and Abdulbhai's son, Arshad, in handcuffs and Farhad's little son.

REGINA

DCP Sharma, please take the handcuffs off. *(Addresses the older Farhad)* Did you set up the bomb and the trigger, Farhadbhai?

FARHAD

(takes his own time answering and shrugs)

Maybe.

REGINA

Only you can save the city now, Farhadbhai. In the name of Islam, in the name of all-merciful and all-compassionate Allah, in the name of the Prophet, in the name of our beloved city, tell us which is the critical wire? Or else your wife will be a widow and you and your son dead in the next two minutes and fourteen seconds, along with God knows how many Mumbai residents.

FARHAD

What do I get in return for saving Mumbai? For the thousands of Muslims in Kashmir, Gujarat and in this city who have been massacred?

REGINA

As God is my witness, you and your brother-in-law will go scot-free and we'll do everything possible to ensure that justice prevails.

FARHAD

Why should I trust you? You're a policewoman.

REGINA

I can only give you my word of honour.

FARHAD

(moves towards the timer)

Your word had better be good. Snap the blue wire.

REGINA

(Mahindra Varma hands her a pair of scissors. She points to the blue wire.)

This one?

FARHAD

(softly)

Yes.

She looks steadily into Farhad's eyes. You can hear the timer ticking. It's the last eleven seconds to midnight. Regina looks intently at the jumble of wires and cuts the green one. Everybody gasps. The timer reaches twelve midnight. There's a split second of silence and then the timer stops ticking and the gas is cut off.

SCENE 128

Int. Day. DGP Goray's office.

DGP Goray and Regina bending down and looking at a spread of Indian newspapers and magazines. Rani's and Regina's pictures on all of them. Rani's name appears, however, as Tarini Raje. The banner headlines read: Tarini and Regina save Bombay. *Second headline:* ACP Regina Fielding and Tarini Raje save a million homes. *Third headline:* Bombay salutes Tarini and Regina as they save a million lives. *Fourth headline:* Apocalypse averted. Tarini and Regina save Mumbai.

DGP GORAY

Isn't her name Rani?

REGINA

That's her pet name. We thought it best to go back to her original name since both the underworld and the politicos are after Rani.

DGP GORAY

And the surname?

REGINA

Her mother was a Raje before marriage.

DGP GORAY

What are we going to do with her now that she's an international superstar? Can't be the saviour of a million one day and Black Tulip the next.

SCENE 129

Int. Day. Regina's office.

Rani and Anzar are sitting at Regina's desk. The scene is shot to make the room look very, very large and the two of them are dwarfed and overwhelmed. They are distinctly uneasy. Regina comes in from a connecting door. She's in her uniform and looks stern and very official. She puts her baton down on the table, pulls her chair back, picks up some papers marked urgent and looks at them. She then calls her secretary on the phone.

REGINA

Ask the DGP if I may come and see him in ten minutes. *(Finally she looks at Rani and Anzar.)* You are looking at a minimum sentence of fifteen years, Rani. It could be thirty. As for you, Anzar Akhtar, seventeen to thirty-five years, R.I.

The blood drains from Rani's face. She's silent. Anzar looks stunned.

ANZAR

R.I.? What for?

REGINA

Hacking into the firewalls of several companies. Your excuse was that you were proving that the firewalls were not failsafe. Unfortunately, hacking is hacking and I believe it's illegal.

Anzar keeps looking at the carpet. Rani takes his hand in hers.

REGINA

(very official)

Will you excuse me now? I've an appointment.

(Regina waits till they are at the visitors' door.)

There is one alternative … the kind where the cure is worse than the disease.

Rani and Anzar are about to leave but stop to listen. Anzar opens the door.

REGINA

You could join the police.

RANI

The police force?

REGINA

I told you, you wouldn't care for it.

RANI

I have no qualifications.

REGINA

Oh yes, you have. A BA in economics and one of the best criminal minds in the business. No one can tell a decoy from the real thing like you.

RANI

What would I have to do?

REGINA

You do the IPS exam and become a DCP, then CP, then IGP and then DGP.

RANI

I'm past the age for the IPS exam.

REGINA

(shaking her head)

Not for a couple of years, at least.

RANI

What about Black Tulip?

Regina opens the drawer of her table and pulls out a couple of afternoon dailies, Mid-day/Afternoon Despatch and Courier. *The headline reads:* Black Tulip killed in police encounter.

REGINA

There's one other condition. *(Rani becomes utterly still. Camera closes in on her face when you hear Regina's next sentence.)* You return all the money stashed in your overseas accounts.

RANI

Live on a DCP's salary?

REGINA

You still have a one-third share in Anzar's venture. He will continue to write the most failsafe and foolproof industrial security software and make millions.

RANI

(looks stricken)

Is there no other way?

REGINA

You could choose jail.

SCENE 130

Int. Day. Office of the Director General of Police.

Regina salutes DGP Goray. Rani and Anzar stay in the background.

DGP

I'm recommending you for the highest gallantry award in the country.

REGINA

Not me, sir. No single person has ever saved as many people as Tarini.

DGP

Welcome to the force, Tarini Raje.

REGINA

And this is Anzar Akhtar.

DGP

Is it true you are the best hacker in the country?

For once Anzar is not sure how to take the compliment.

ANZAR

I'm not bad, sir.

REGINA

He's being modest.

DCP Sharma knocks but does not wait for an answer.

DCP SHARMA

Forgive the interruption, sir. The minister's on TV.

DCP Sharma switches on the TV.

MINISTER

Two weeks ago I promised that I would clear this city of crime. I've kept my promise. Four days ago this city was faced with total extinction. Explosives would have killed 60,000 cricket fans at the one-day match at the Wankhede Stadium. But there was much worse to come. Mumbai city would have gone up in flames and killed at least a million people. But the danger has been averted. I wish to thank the police department for its work.

DCP SHARMA

The minister also wanted me to deliver this envelope to ACP Fielding right away.

DCP Sharma hands the envelope to Regina. Regina tears the envelope and reads the letter.

REGINA

I've got my marching orders. I've been posted to Amravati.

There's a stunned silence in the room.

SCENE 131

Int. Evening. Minister Sane's office.

MINISTER SANE

What is it, Goray? I've a tight schedule and a flight to Delhi at eight.

DGP GORAY

This will take only a minute, sir. It's about ACP Regina Fielding.

MINISTER SANE

What about her? She has been moved to Amravati now.

DGP GORAY

That's the point, sir.

MINISTER SANE

I take the decisions here, Goray. Please remember that.

DGP GORAY

I never forget it, sir. But if we transfer her now, there will be a furore in the press. And the Centre may not take kindly to it.

MINISTER SANE

As if I give a damn. What do you suggest then?

DGP GORAY

Why not put her where she has a zero profile?

MINISTER SANE

And where would that be?

DGP GORAY

One of her minor responsibilities was to set up a cyber crimes cell. She doesn't have a clue about computers or Internet crimes. *(Smiles foxily)* Why not let her run that show full-time?

MINISTER SANE

Just so long as the press and the public never hear of her again.

SCENE 132

Int. Day. Minister Sane's office.

DGP Goray, ACP Regina and Rani enter. Rani's in uniform.

MINISTER

Congratulations Fielding, you are now Joint Commissioner of Police. This city is not likely to forget its debt to you.

REGINA

Thank you, Minister. Thank you for the assistance and guidance you've given me during my stay here.

MINISTER

All the best in the cyber crimes division.

DGP GORAY

I wanted to introduce you to our new Deputy Commissioner of Police, sir.

Rani salutes the minister smartly.

RANI

Afternoon, sir. Rani reporting for duty

The minister's cell phone rings. Close-up of red cellphone. He switches it on.

MINISTER

Not now. I'm busy. Try me after half an hour.

MINISTER

(a little shaken)

Rani?

REGINA

Tarini, sir.

MINISTER

For a moment I thought it was the Black Tulip.

DGP GORAY

Where did you get that idea, sir? She's long dead. Tarini's going to watch over you in Nasik.

MINISTER

Watch over me?

DGP

Look after your safety.

MINISTER

I'll look forward to having a beautiful officer look after me.

RANI

Pleasure, sir.

SCENE 133

Ext. Day. In Regina's car.

Rani's got the minister's red mobile phone in her hand.

REGINA

You didn't.

Rani smiles and plugs the cellphone to a gadget that copies all the numbers and other information from the minister's phone.

RANI

There. Now we have all the secret numbers he calls on the mobile with the false identity.

REGINA

You are incorrigible.

RANI

(smiles)

Oops, I forgot my briefcase in his office.

Cut to the minister's office.

RANI

Forgive me, sir, I forgot my briefcase.

While picking up her briefcase, Rani puts the phone on his desk without the minister noticing. The cellphone rings and the minister picks it up. He waits for her to close the door but Rani is listening before closing the door.

MINISTER

Yes, Saleh?

SCENE 134

Int. Day. The computer division.

Regina and Rani are standing next to Anzar who is working at a computer.

REGINA

How are we doing?

ANZAR

I am close but it will still take a few days to crack the code of Saleh's and Minister Sane's money-laundering operations.

DCP Khan enters brusquely and goes straight to Regina.

DCP KHAN

You won't believe this but there's a copy-cat at work.

She switches on the TV.

NEWSREADER

Mafia boss Saleh got a taste of his own medicine when he engaged one of the most sought-after hairdressers and make-up artists in the country for his daughter's wedding to the scion of a former cricket captain from Pakistan. The bride looked stunning in what turned out to be fake jewellery since the orignal was stolen from under her nose and that too from her own father's home. We hear Salehbhai is furious and his men are hunting for the culprit but so far without success.

REGINA

(looks at Rani, trying to process the information; her voice clouds over with doubt.)

Copycat?

THE END

THE OTHER ENDING

SCENE 94

Ext. Night. Police Headquarters, DGP Goray's office

Regina knocks on DGP Goray's door in Police HQ.

DGP GORAY

Come in. Any luck?

REGINA

No, sir.

DGP GORAY

That should be good news but whoever's behind this is not going to let us off that easy.

REGINA

May I speak out of turn, sir?

DGP GORAY

What's on your mind, Fielding?

REGINA

You had said in your first briefing on Operation Agatha that we should go by our gut feeling.

DGP GORAY

And what's your gut feeling?

REGINA

Let's cancel tomorrow's cricket match at Wankhede.

DGP GORAY

But you've already been over the place thrice, I was told.

REGINA

I did and found nothing.

DGP GORAY

And you still want to cancel the match? *(Looks a long time at her)* I love this city a little more than I hate what it's become. We've got to save it for our children. Let's go and see the minister.

SCENE 95

Int. Midnight. Minister Sane's bungalow.

MINISTER SANE

(comes out, buttoning his kurta)

You better have a damn good reason to wake me up so late at night.

REGINA

I've come to ask you to cancel tomorrow's match at the Wankhede Stadium.

MINISTER SANE

On what grounds?

REGINA

It is the most likely target of the attack…

MINISTER SANE

I asked a straightforward question. I want a straightforward answer. Do you you have any evidence?

REGINA

Just a gut feeling, sir.

MINISTER SANE

(turns to DGP Goray)

You woke me up at midnight to cancel the most eagerly awaited sports event of the year because some clown under you had nothing better than a gut feeling about a terrorist attack? *(Pause)*

ACP Regina, you are dismissed from the police force with immediate effect and, as for you, DGP Goray I'll have you stripped of your rank and disgraced in public. Now get out before I call the security guards to evict you.

SCENE 96

Int. Night. Rani's apartment.

The cellphone rings. It's past midnight. Rani rushes into the kitchen and closes the door since Anzar is fast asleep.

RANI

Yes, Jehan.

JEHAN

You said I should call if I remembered anything.

RANI

Tell me.

JEHAN

My brother-in-law, Farhad, said that tomorrow's game of cricket would be lots of fun and fireworks and make this the best Diwali ever.

RANI

Where is he?

JEHAN

My brother and he left for Dubai.

RANI

They didn't wait for your father's funeral?

JEHAN

They had some urgent business but they'll be back day-after morning when the police release the body from the morgue.

SCENE 97

Ext. Morning 9 a.m. Outside the Police HQ at Crawford Market.

Regina addressing DCP Karan Sharma, DCP Bilquis Khan, Inspector Lily Pinto and other senior police officers.

REGINA

As of last night, Minister Sane dismissed me from the force. *(Total silence and shock)*. But that is not the issue just now. I have a major favour to ask of you. *(DGP Goray has joined the others)* Will you go back to Wankhede Stadium and go over every centimetre of ground there? The match starts at 2 pm. You have very little time.

DCP SHARMA

But we examined every inch of the place yesterday.

REGINA

You are under no compulsion to take instructions from me.

SCENE 98

Ext. Day. Wankhede Stadium.

DGP Goray, CP Ghosh, CP Roongta, Bilquis, Inspector Pinto and several inspectors and constables are checking the premises. Cut to Regina, sitting outside the stadium. DCP Sharma rushes to CP Ghosh.

DCP SHARMA

The crowds are screaming to be let in, sir.

Cut to the crowds outside. Cut back to earlier conversation.

CP GHOSH

Ten more minutes.

DCP SHARMA

You've been saying that for the past hour, sir.

CP GHOSH

Find the RDX, DCP Sharma.

Cut to a view of the stadium with police personnel at various levels of the stadium and also under it.

DCP KHAN

Minister Sane is on his way and wants to know why we haven't let the crowds in yet.

CP GHOSH

(swearing)

Should we warn him that the RDX might just go off under his butt?

BILQUIS

(suppressing a smile)

I will convey that to him, sir.

Just then Inspector Pinto who has been checking one of the steel towers that support the bank of lights comes over to DGP Goray and CP Ghosh.

INSPECTOR PINTO

(softly)

Will you come with me, sir?

Cut to one of the horizontal right-angled beams supporting the roof in which a timer device is quietly ticking away. Cut to a number of policemen scouring every nook and corner under and in the stadium and tracing the wires and the plastic explosives. Cut to the crowds trying to break through the cordon of police. Cut to the first ball of the match being bowled. Cut to Regina slumped in relief outside the stadium.

DGP GORAY

(to Inspector Pinto)

The RDX circuitry seems to have the hallmark of Salehbhai's work. Which means that the Indian Mujahideen hired him to run the operation for them. Have the plastic explosives sent to the lab for analysis. *(To Bilquis Khan and the DCPs)* Round up each and every one of Salehbhai's men from the city.

SCENE 99

Int. Evening. Minister Sane's office.

MINISTER SANE

What is it, Goray? I've a tight schedule and a flight to Delhi at eight.

DGP GORAY

We now know that Salehbhai was the mastermind behind the planned attack. But the job was outsourced to him by the Indian Mujahideen. They were the ones who planted the RDX.

MINISTER SANE

Are you finished with your report?

DGP GORAY

Just one thing, sir. It's about ACP Regina Fielding.

MINISTER SANE

What about her? She's no longer with the force. And as soon as I come back from Delhi you too will be in for a few unpleasant surprises.

REGINA

Perhaps you might want to watch a video uploaded on YouTube.

MINISTER SANE

I have no time for such frivolity.

His cellphone registers an SMS. Cut to the message. 'Go to YouTube. You might find yourself out of a job.' *Cut to close-up of YouTube of the session where Minister Sane sacks Regina and demotes DGP Goray.*

SCENE 100

Ext. Night. Home Minister Sane's large backyard.

A press conference is in progress.

MINISTER SANE

There are some mischievous elements who have sought to cast doubts on our Mumbai Police by uploading a fake video on YouTube. I wish to emphasize in the strongest manner possible that I stand solidly behind ACP Regina Fielding. She has shown exceptional wisdom and bravery in the face of the gravest danger to our city. As of now, she will be promoted to Joint Commissioner of Police. As for DGP Goray, I am recommending him for the highest possible award in the police service. Their instructions are to bring the criminals behind the attempted terrorist attack on Wankhede Stadium to book at the earliest.

SCENE 101

Int. Evening. Regina's home.

REGINA

Your options are limited. Either you go to jail. Or you freelance for me till you take your IPS exams.

RANI

How do I make a living?

REGINA

You've handed over most of your ill-begotten wealth but I think you kept aside a little nest egg. So live off it unless you want me to report to the tax people.

RANI

(a little shamefaced)

This is blackmail.

REGINA

You bet. Besides, Anzar is still freelancing after-hours. That thirty-three and one-third per cent could still keep you flush.

RANI

What about work?

REGINA

I'm reserving you for special ops. Keep a low profile. Zero profile is better.

SCENE 102

Int. Day. Regina's office.

REGINA

(addressing all the police officers under her)

I can never get over the Shishupal story. Lord Krishna waited patiently until Shishupal had committed a hundred crimes and then, that was it. He terminated him. Saleh is way past the hundred mark. Seventy thousand would have died at the stadium. And don't forget Bijlee. Shall we get him or will he go scot-free?

SCENE 103

Int. Night. Rani's apartment.

Rani and Anzar are having dinner in the kitchen. He has a black mourning band around his left sleeve.

RANI

Special ops. What kind of surgery does she want me to perform?

ANZAR

It's got nothing to do with surgery, stupid.

RANI

(sarcastic)

Oh, thank you for enlightening me.

ANZAR

You're welcome. After all, what are friends for?

RANI

Smartarse. Who are you mourning?

ANZAR

(his voice is shaky and his right hand goes to his forehead in a melodramatic gesture of mourning)

My life's no longer worth living. The grapevine says my fiancée and my dowry have both dumped me.

RANI

Who's the heiress this time? Bill Gate's daughter?

ANZAR

Ha, that's chickenfeed. Salehbhai's daughter, Azeeza. Bhai's coughing up over fifty crore and jewellery worth the same amount as dowry for her. The Moghul jewellery is showcased in this month's *Vogue*.

RANI

You would have ditched me for a mere fifty crore? Shame on you.

ANZAR

Let me give you some advice. Money, my dear, is not everything. *(Pause)* It is the only thing.

RANI

I'm bored, Anzar. I'm suffering from acute withdrawal symptoms.

SCENE 104

Int. Day. A posh hairdressing school.

Ms Sangita is standing in front of a blackboard with various kinds of women's faces drawn on it: one round, one plump, one with extremely angular chin and jaws, one with an overlong face. Another series with large beautiful eyes, eyes excessively close to each other, small eyes. Another row with a variety of noses, another with different kinds of ears and yet another with varying foreheads, narrow, very big, receding, one with a widow's peak, and so on.

SANGITA

The face is the canvas in our profession whether it's flawless or full of flaws. Study your client's face. Identify its strengths and weaknesses. Now use science and technology to improve upon God's work.

You hear part of Ms Sangita's speech as Rani works on a plaster bust of a woman with curly hair on a pedestal in front of her.

SCENE 105

Int. Night. Rani's drawing room.

The TV is on and you see a newspaper headline from a paper called Glam And Glitz: Incognito Saudi Princess highest paid hairdresser for brides in the world.

V.O.

Saudi Princess-cum-face artist who prefers to be anonymous says there's no such thing as ugly. Give me any face and I will turn it into a work of art.

A series of before-and-after pictures of women appear on the TV screen.

Camera recedes to show Rani still working on the hair of the plaster bust of the woman. She looks frustrated.

RANI

I'm never going to get this right.

SCENE 106

Ext. Noon. Dubai Airport.

A woman in a black burkha with a veil that covers the whole face barring the eyes walks out of the airport. She looks around and sees a driver dressed in a white uniform and a cap with a placard that says 'Lady Aka'. Behind the driver is a young woman who is also in a burkha. The heavily veiled lady walks up to the driver and is greeted by the young woman.

AZEEZA

(tentatively)

Lady Aka?

LADY AKA

You must be Azeeza.

(they sit in the car)

AZEEZA

Highness, I'm so grateful you agreed to come.

LADY AKA

Just Madam Aka will do. I promised my father I will never be recognized and bring dishonour to our family.

AZEEZA

Your husband, does he object to your being a beautician?

LADY AKA

He divorced me a long time ago. He wanted a younger beauty who would bear him a male heir.

AZEEZA

How odd, my father left my mother for the same reason.

SCENE 107

Int. Evening. Azeeza's luxurious home.

Aka is still in a partial veil and you still can't make out her features. She's delicately drawing a highly complex lace design with henna paste on Azeeza's hands and feet.

AZEEZA

Do you like your suite?

AKA

Yes, it's fine.

AZEEZA

What a silly question. You live in a palace.

AKA

(smiles)

But not in a triplex. Where are all the guests?

AZEEZA

In the flat across. It's a mad house there. Some of the guests have been put up in hotels. Would you like to see the rest of the house?

AKA

Yes. I'm a sleepwalker. Don't get alarmed if you see me walking into your room in the middle of the night.

Cut to the two walking around the place from floor to floor, and room to room and suite to suite.

AKA

Do you mind if I take your photographs against different backgrounds. It will help me understand your face and how to sculpt it for the nikah.

Aka shoots pictures of Azeeza at various locations in the apartment. Just as they reach Salehbhai's office, he steps out with the boy one had seen with Bijlee. He jumps into Azeeza's arms. She hugs him and kisses him. Aka immediately pulls the full veil over her face.

ALLA RAKHA

Didi, where have you been?

AZEEZA

I went to the airport to pick up Aka auntie, Alla Rakha.

Aka shoots pictures of the two together.

AKA

Hello, Alla Rakha. What's that in your hand?

ALLA RAKHA

It's a video game. You want to play?

AKA

What will you give me if I defeat you?

ALLA RAKHA

(laughs)

Fat chance. I beat Abbajaan nine times out of ten even though he cheats.

Salehbhai greets Aka effusively. He's obviously in awe of royalty.

SALEHBHAI

Welcome to our humble abode, Princess.

AKA

Hardly humble. One request. Our contract stipulated that I should not be called Princess or Highness.

SALEHBHAI

I understand. Your visit here is under wraps.

He opens the door to a huge room with a big working table and a computer. There's a conference table at one end and a bar. And behind it another room.

SALEHBHAI

This is my office. That desktop is the latest and most expensive in the world.

AKA

Very impressive.

SALEHBHAI

I'm a self-made man. Everything you see here, I earned it. Not like you who have been given everything on a platter.

AZEEZA

(embarrassed)

Abbajaan!

SALEHBHAI

It's the truth. And I am proud of it. Let me show you what's behind this door.

He opens a door behind the conference table. It leads to a garishly opulent bedroom with a mirror on the ceiling. He takes Aka to a bathroom with a Jacuzzi and a range of perfumes and expensive cosmetics. Cut to the balcony adjoining the bedroom. It looks out onto the sea.

SALEHBHAI

Can you make this young lady look passable so her husband won't throw her out on her wedding night?

AKA

Your daughter is a lovely young woman.

SALEHBHAI

(laughs)

I had no idea that mousy ladies are in fashion now. *(Azeeza cringes)* Azeeza, you don't need me for the sangeet. I'm going out with your groom and his father to celebrate your wedding.

SCENE 108

Int. Evening. Salehbhai's office.

Alla Rakha and Aka are seated at the big table and playing a game on Salehbhai's fancy computer. When Alla Rakha is concentrating on his next move, Aka is quietly shooting pictures of Alla Rakha and surreptitiously of the computer set-up. Azeeza walks in.

AZEEZA

Today is sangeet. We are going to sing and dance in the courtyard downstairs. Won't you join us?

AKA

I can't. You know the reason.

AZEEZA

But there will be only my friends and relatives. All of them women, except my brother Alla Rakha, of course.

AKA

Yes, but they will be shooting a video and taking photographs. And your friends will want to know why am I not getting rid of my burkha. Can't I watch from up here?

AZEEZA

Of course you can, from the balcony of your suite. *(Pauses)* Did you mean what you told my father? Or were you just flattering me?

AKA

You will find out tomorrow.

AZEEZA

(comes over and kisses Aka on the cheek)

Thank you.

SCENE 109

Int. Night. Inside Princess Aka's suite.

It's past midnight. The flat is silent. Princess Aka steps out of her room and walks up to the office and softly opens the door of the bedroom beyond the conference table. Aka is on her cellphone as she unscrews the back of the desktop. She speaks softly but clearly. She keeps getting instructions and either says 'Done', 'Come again' or 'Roger'. She plants a hacking device with a mike and a camera inside, then puts the screws back into the machine after the job is done.

SCENE 110

Int. Night. Aka's bedroom.

It's around 3 a.m. when Aka hears someone at her bedroom door. Before she can put on the veil covering her nose, Azeeza walks in and quietly lies

down next to Aka, crying silently. It's left to the audience to decide if Azeeza has seen Aka's face. Aka puts her arm around Azeeza and quietens her down, patting her gently.

AKA

What's troubling you, Azeeza?

AZEEZA

What if he throws me out just like my father got rid of my mother?

AKA

Who?

AZEEZA

My fiancé. What if he doesn't like me despite the dowry my father has given him?

AKA

Then it might be better if he divorces you. Imagine being tolerated out of pity. You're educated, you can stand on your own feet and get a job.

AZEEZA

My father always said I was ugly and I had no brains.

AKA

Do you believe him?

AZEEZA

I don't want to.

AKA

No one else can tell you your worth. You decide it for yourself.

SCENE 111

Int. Morning. Azeeza's dressing room.

This scene has to be worked out carefully and must look authentic. Aka has washed Azeeza's hair and is drying it. Cut to Azeeza sitting in front

of a mirror with a central panel and two side panels, all of which are covered with a cloth like a bedsheet. A video camera is shooting the session. As usual Alla Rakha is hanging on to Azeeza.

AZEEZA

Can't I watch what you are doing?

AKA

(shakes her head)

Trust me.

AZEEZA

Then how will I learn all your secrets?

AKA

No secrets. The video will show you exactly what I am doing. Besides, I never do anything so complicated that you can't reproduce it.

Aka is working steadily but with deft fingers and a sureness of touch creating an artwork in front of our eyes. She dresses Azeeza in her bridal clothes. Aka doesn't care for the dupatta Azeeza has chosen, and goes through the whole collection of Azeeza's dupattas to select a pastel shade. One by one, she lifts the pieces of jewellery from the dressing table and adorns Azeeza with the different items. The last piece is the priceless necklace with a locket.

ALLA RAKHA

Didi, you look so beautiful.

Aka hooks the necklace firmly around Azeeza's neck now. A couple of final touches and the bride is ready. Aka removes the curtains from the mirrors. Azeeza looks at the woman in the mirror. She's the same and yet, she is so different. Aka's work is low-key. She might have changed the parting in Azeeza hair and highlighted a few features differently but she has exploited Azeeza's features to their full potential and turned Azeeza into an aristocratic lady with a lovely face and even more important, imbued her with poise and inner self-confidence.

AZEEZA

(gets up slowly and hugs Aka)

How did you do it?

AKA

No magic. It was all there. I merely highlighted it.

AZEEZA

How can I ever thank you?

SCENE 112

Int. Day. Aka's suite

Aka taking her leave. The servants have already taken her luggage down.

AZEEZA

Please stay for my wedding. I owe you so much.

AKA

I'm sorry I can't. I wish you the very best, Azeeza.

Azeeza kisses Aka on her cheeks and leaves.

SCENE 113

Int. Evening. Regina's flat.

Newspapers are lying all over the place. 'Mafia boss loses face and 50 crore worth jewellery.' 'Copycat Black Tulip steals diamond necklace worth fifteen million dollars from Bhai.' *Rani, Regina and Anzar are sitting in the drawing room, having drinks. Regina is scrutinizing the jewellery on the table.*

REGINA

(shaking her head in wonderment, smiling)

Cheers. *(Hugs Rani)* You did what the entire police force couldn't. Not just me, this city owes you big time.

ANZAR

Plus, now we can track Salehbhai's every move. And hopefully put him behind bars forever.

REGINA

I'm putting you in a safehouse tonight, Rani. You will not stir out for a month.

RANI

You can't be serious.

REGINA

You will have 24/7 security. You will study at home, pass the IPS exams and start assisting me.

ANZAR

Am I allowed to visit her?

REGINA

Maybe later. Lest I forget, we're not letting on that the police have recovered the Moghul diamond set.

SCENE 114

Int. Midnight. Outside Regina's office.

Anzar is pacing up and down the balcony-like passage leading to Regina's office. Regina steps out of her car and rushes up to the first floor. Bilquis is waiting for her in her office.

REGINA

What do you mean she's missing? What about the security guards?

ANZAR

They've been bumped off.

REGINA

You checked every room?

ANZAR

Yes. Over and over again.

BILQUIS

Any sign of a scuffle?

ANZAR

Not that I noticed.

REGINA

Give Bilquis the keys. *(To Bilquis)* Wear an expensive sari and pretend you're visiting one of Rani's neighbours. Check for fingerprints and clues. Pack a gun with you. Come back safe. *(Bilquis leaves.)*

ANZAR

Do you suspect anybody particular in your department?

REGINA

Every single person starting with you and me.

SCENE 115

Int. Night. Interior. Salehbhai's cabin in his luxury yacht.

Rani is on the floor. She has been beaten badly, and is all bruised and bloody. Her left eye is swollen and closed.

SALEH

I'm in no hurry, bitch. I've got all the time in the world till you tell me where the jewels are.

RANI

What jewels?

Saleh kicks her.

SALEH

The ones you stole from Azeeza.

RANI

Who's Azeeza?

SALEH

(kicking her again)

This one's from Azeeza. And this one's from me.

SCENE 116

Int. Day. Anzar's small office adjoining Regina's.

REGINA

(peeping in)

Any luck with Bhai's emails?

ANZAR

I'm not sure but there's one message sent on the day Rani disappeared which is intriguing. It just says 'Thank you'. Other messages from the same source follow. The last one today says, 'Launch will pick you up tomorrow at the Gateway at 8 pm.'

REGINA

Who's the recipient?

ANZAR

The address is obviously a fake one. It's taken me all night but I've finally traced it to one Karan Sharma.

REGINA

(doesn't react but something's clicked)

That figures. It's the same officer who revealed Bijlee's name to the press. Sharma pretended to be contrite when Saleh killed her and offered to resign. Smart move. I bought into it. Can we send an email to the same address without him tracing it to our email address?

ANZAR

Yes.

REGINA

(reads)

Dear DCP Sharma,
I've just recommended your name to the governor in this year's honours list. Brilliant, the way you inveigled yourself into the enemy camp, won their confidence and planted false information about B.T. Congratulations.

ANZAR

(digests the information and nods)

Why didn't I think of that?

REGINA

Both Saleh and we will watch him 24/7 from now on. He'll either report this email to me or he'll turn up at the Gateway tomorrow.

ANZAR

May I ask you something?

REGINA

(wary)

Go ahead.

ANZAR

We both know it's already too late, don't we?

Regina is lost in thought for a long time till Anzar becomes uncomfortable. It's clear that she's hurting but tries not to show it.

REGINA

You worked for a full three months to set up the story of the incognito Saudi Arabian princess. We both thought we had a foolproof plan.

ANZAR

It was.

REGINA

Yes, but one of the police officers turned out to be Saleh's man. Sometimes I'm forced to knowingly put other people's lives at risk.

Collateral damage they call it. *(She looks away)* My excuse was that we wanted to catch Bhai at any cost. But there's no forgiveness for such decisions when they go wrong. We better make sure Rani comes out of this alive and whole.

ANZAR

What if I spread the word on Facebook that a mole from the police double-crossed Bhai by telling him it was a copycat Black Tulip who had stolen the Ranjit Singh jewels.

REGINA

(smiles)

Not bad, not bad at all.

SCENE 117

Int. Night. Regina's office.

Anzar knocks on the door.

REGINA

Yes?

ANZAR

(walking in)

Any news?

REGINA

No. Sharma seems to have gone missing.

ANZAR

Do we know the location of Bhai's yacht?

REGINA

The coast guard has tracked him down. His luxury yacht is parked just outside Indian waters.

ANZAR

Can't we board it and rescue Rani?

REGINA

And create an international incident? Instead, why don't you think of a way to get the yacht into Indian waters?

ANZAR

Will you tell the coast guard to give us all the dope on the yacht?

REGINA

Like what?

ANZAR

The make, its communication systems, the computer in the captain's cabin.

SCENE 118

Int. Night. Salehbhai's cabin on the yacht.

SALEHBHAI

Are you telling me ACP Karan Sharma was neither at the Gateway nor at home?

ABDUL

He wasn't.

SALEHBHAI

So where the fuck is he?

ABDUL

The word in the market is that DCP Karan Sharma played us dirty.

SCENE 119

Int. Night. The hold of Salehbhai's yacht.

Salehbhai enters and switches on the light. Rani's on the floor. She is black and blue and trussed up with her hands and feet tied behind her.

SALEHBHAI

I've news for you. Azeeza's coming over to identify you. *(Laughs theatrically)* Abdul, take her to the guestroom and let her shower.

SCENE 120

Int. Morning. The drawing room in the yacht.

Azeeza arrives on a small motorboat. Cut to Rani sitting in a semi-comatose state on the sofa.

SALEHBHAI

Where's Alla Rakha?

AZEEZA

At the wheel in the captain's cabin.

SALEHBHAI

(raises Rani's chin)

You recognize her, right? It's because of you we hired this impostor pretending to be a Saudi princess. She's the one who was your stylist, yes?

AZEEZA

(looks at Rani for a long time)

You've reconfigured her and expect me to recognize her?

SALEHBHAI

Yes or no?

AZEEZA

(goes over Rani's face again and looks into her eyes)

No. The princess was older. *(Opens a bottle in her purse and hands over a pill to Rani)* Take this aspirin. *(She feeds Rani the pill and then holds a glass of water to her lips and leaves the bottle on a table.)* It will reduce the pain and the swelling. Abdul, give her tea and a good breakfast.

SCENE 121

Int. Noon. The captain's cabin.

AZEEZA

Come, Alla Rakha. I'm taking you home.

SALEHBHAI

He stays here.

AZEEZA

I don't want him to stay here with you.

SALEHBHAI

I don't recall asking for your advice. Go to your husband before he throws you out.

SCENE 122

Ext. Night. The prow of the yacht.

Salehbhai standing at the prow with Rani on the floor beside him. From the direction of the Gateway of India a small coast guard vessel proceeds towards Salehbhai. The floodlights from the luxury yacht light up Bilquis as the coast guard boat comes to a halt. Some of Salehbhai's gang members are standing, watching the show. A tourist boat blaring music and carrying a raucous group of people passes close by on its way to the Gateway of India. The men and women on the boat are waving out to Saleh and a couple of his men. Saleh watches them with ill-concealed disgust. From the other side of the passing tourist boat, four coast guards and Regina jump over and dive underwater. One of the coast guards throws a line with a steel hook on the railing of Salehbhai's yacht. Its clatter is drowned out in the racket the tourist boat is making. At the back of the yacht the four members of the coast guard are helping Regina over the railing. During the following scene there are quick cuts between the coastguards overpowering Salehbhai's men in the control room and in the engine room one by one, gagging them and tying them up. Regina shoves her gun into the captain's back and shows him her police identity card and puts her finger on her lips.

REGINA

(whispering)

Say just one word and I'll blow your brains out.

(Cut to Salehbhai)

SALEH

(talking to Bilquis Khan)

Where's your boss lady, that Anglo dame?

BILQUIS

She's busy.

SALEH

(pulling Rani up by her hair)

Recognize this little bitch here.

BILQUIS

Who's that?

SALEH

Black Tulip.

BILQUIS

(laughs)

You can't be serious. She died some months ago in a police encounter.

SALEH

(looks uncertain for a moment, then regains his bravado)

Sure, maybe that's why she reincarnated as a police agent.

BILQUIS

I see that your imagination is hyperactive.

SALEH

(places a knife at Rani's throat)

Cut out the crap. Tell your boss lady if she's not here within ten minutes this bitch will be dead. Call now.

Bilquis shrugs her shoulders, dials a number and talks to Regina who's standing in the cockpit behind transparent glass windows from where she can see Salehbhai.

BILQUIS

Ma'am, Salehbhai says if you are not here within ten minutes, he will kill a hostage who he claims is Black Tulip. *(Bilquis listens on the*

mobile and repeats what she has been told) She says if you want to kill Black Tulip a second time, it's fine with her.

SALEH

Tell her I'm willing to cut a deal.

BILQUIS

(listens on the phone and repeats)

What kind of deal?

SALEH

The diamond necklace set in exchange for Black Tulip.

BILQUIS

Why would we be talking to you if we had the necklace set which you stole?

SALEHBHAI

I didn't steal it. I bought the set at a phenomenal price.

BILQUIS

But you knew it's a prized national heritage item.

SALEH

Enough talk or I will kill the bitch.

Regina steps out of the cabin as the coast guard in the cockpit switches on all the lights and four coast guard boats train their floodlights on Salehbhai.

REGINA

No deal. Drop the knife and let the woman go.

SALEH

Aha, the boss lady in person. You're trespassing. Get off my yacht. This minute.

REGINA

Wrong. You're in Indian territory.

SALEHBHAI

Bullshit. We're in international waters.

REGINA

You are half a mile inside Indian waters now.

SALEH

(yells)

Captain, tell this bloody policewoman that she's on my boat and in international waters.

The captain comes out of the navigation room escorted by the coast guards.

CAPTAIN

I'm sorry, sir, we seem to have drifted into Indian territory.

SALEH

Drifted? What the fuck were you doing?

CAPTAIN

I think our navigational system was hacked.

SALEH

Tell you what I'm going to do, Captain. Hack you to pieces along with this lady here.

He grabs Rani. Alla Rakha, who has been watching all along from the roof of the captain's cabin, jumps down the roof and runs to Regina, calling out her name. Salehbhai is about to slit Rani's throat when he sees his son in Regina's arms. He throws Rani down with great force and grabs Alla Rakha. Rani falls on the floor in a heap and pretends to have passed out.

SALEHBHAI

(holding his gun to Alla Rakha's head)

Listen carefully, policewoman. Get the jewels, you bitch, or I'll kill this boy. No kidding.

Rani has drawn the knife close to her with her foot.

REGINA

Let Alla Rakha go, Salehbhai. He's your son.

SALEHBHAI

I will, after you hand over the jewels. Every one of them.

Rani leaps up and kicks Saleh hard behind the knee so that he falls down. Regina grabs the boy and turns his head away. Salehbhai reaches for his fallen gun when Rani stabs his arm which spurts like a geyser and he screams in pain. Rani grabs the gun.

REGINA

Don't, Rani, I beg you, don't.

RANI

(shoves the gun hard in his mouth and is about to squeeze the trigger but changes her mind)

How does it feel to be at the receiving end?

She throws the gun at one of the coast guards who catches it.

SCENE 123

Ext. Midnight. Gateway of India.

Salehbhai is escorted handcuffed to the shore from his yacht. Regina follows with Alla Rakha and then offers Rani a hand. Rani ignores the proffered hand. Anzar is waiting for Rani. Rani walks on to the shore and past him. He runs after her.

ANZAR

Rani. Rani, wait.

She turns to look at him a long time and then continues to walk away. Anzar turns to Regina.

REGINA

(shaking her head)

Let her be, Anzar. Whatever Bhai did to her couldn't have been easy. Give her time and pray for her.

Rani walks into the distance all alone.

THE END

AFTERWORD

One of my earliest memories is of a movie called *Highway 301* which was to be released at Aurora cinema in the suburb of Matunga in Mumbai. Now, it's quite routine to remember films one has seen but I suspect the reason *Highway 301* left such a strong impression on me was because while it was talked about a great deal, there was no way I would have been allowed to see it. It had got an 'A' certificate and the grapevine reported that the Central Board of Film Certification (CBFC) had not only butchered the film but was still debating whether *Highway 301* should be given permission to be exhibited. Finally, after a lot of back and forth, the CBFC made up its mind. No, the film was not suitable for those below eighteen and all those above. Please remember we are talking about the very early 1950s when the CBFC was assiduously vigilant about the morals of a subcontinent that had just won independence and it was believed that Indians needed to be saved from the corrupting influence of the West.[1]

With all that hullabaloo surrounding the film, *Highway 301* had become more tempting for me than the apple Eve offered Adam, but luckily the astral entity called the CBFC had managed to save me from

---

[1]That belief has been operative for nearly seventy years now and has of late shown signs of becoming more virulent. As late as August 2014, the CBFC was still spending time arguing whether 'I'm still a virgin' should be snipped off. The ruling ethos veers more and more towards intolerance and censorship. By culture we no longer mean the various religious and secular, literary, philosophical, theatre, dance, artistic, mythological traditions that have enriched our lives but a single homogenous entity as promulgated by the powers that be. The saddest part of this exercise is that the very notion of openness, which is the hallmark of the majority religion, is under severe threat.

rack and ruination. As it turned out, not for long though. I was destined to be depraved and damned for good because a couple of years later, *Highway 301* was released at Aurora and that too with a 'U' certificate. The film had been sanitized to the extent that it was now safe to expose even five-month-old foetuses to it. Needless to say, it was impossible to make head or tail of the goings-on in the film. But there was no denying that *Highway 301* turned out to be my first encounter with a film that centred on a robbery. Only years later would I learn that it belonged to a genre called 'film noir'.

The two films which many critics believe are the definitive pioneers of the heist-film genre are Jules Dassin's *Rififi* (1954) and Jean-Pierre Melville's *Bob le Flambeur (1956)*. The archetypal *Rififi* has a rivetting, edge-of-the-seat, twenty-four-minute silent robbery sequence. Dassin also made the caper *Topkapi* in 1964 in which the heist revolves around the Ottoman Emperor's dagger. The film starred his wife Melina Mercouri, Maximillian Schell, Peter Ustinov and Robert Morley. *Gambit* was another caper that has stayed in my mind and then there was *The Great Train Robbery* based on Michael Crichton's delightful book of the same name. These capers were almost always laced with humour and involved a group of three or four people working together to pull off a robbery. As heist comedies go, I haven't seen anything half as funny as *A Fish Called Wanda*. (I have to hang my head in shame and confess that if you were to show *Wanda* to me again after a record of thirteen viewings, I give you my word I'll once again be rolling on the floor and will very likely be put behind bars for making a public nuisance of myself.)

After the 1990s the nature of the heist movie changed radically. Its inspiration was high-tech and both characterization and humour took an almost lethal hit. *Mission Impossible* and *Entrapment* could be cited as two examples of this.

I suspect *Black Tulip* carves out its own unique space because Rani, the thief in my script, operates entirely on her own and does so without any mechanical, digital or electronic gadgetry. All she has is her wits and an acting talent which helps her impersonate different characters.

Screenplay Writing and Me

I started writing screenplays around the time I wrote my first play, *Bedtime Story*, in 1976. As readers of my novel *Ravan and Eddie* will tell you, that project began as a screenplay when a director with a powerful film to his credit asked me to write something for him. I suspect he had had second-hand experience of my Marathi novel *Saat Sakkam Trechalis* since he didn't know Marathi and must have thought that I would write either an exposé or a searing indictment of our society. By the time we met for the third time, maybe it was the second, he dropped me without as much a by-your-leave.

I owe the director a great deal for not pursuing the project for I realized later that we did not share any common ground or a similar way of looking at the world. He was earnest and serious-bordering-on-the-solemn and had a fondness for the melodramatic and for that laboured Indian institution called a message. I, on the other hand, like to puncture my pretence of aspiring to loftier heights with black humour, ribaldry and self-deprecation. Perhaps we both did each other a favour. But in one particular area he had set the pattern. So far my experience has been that film people come over, talk to me, even engage my services and then disappear without notice.

Since *Ravan and Eddie*, I have written another five or six screenplays and warmed them under my seat for years though no egg gets hatched. As I don't move about in film circles (not that I move in literary circles either), I've hardly ever shown my scripts to anybody. But since the time when my novel *Saat Sakkam Trechalis* was translated into English as *Seven Sixes Are Forty-three*, big and small producers and directors have approached me to allow them to convert every single novel of mine into a film. They keep harping on the 'crying need' for screenplays of substance and depth and how most novels do not lend themselves to a transition to films whereas my work, they feel, is made for the medium. I am sure that initially it inflated my ego to have people asking me for the rights to my work. But that euphoria faded away rather rapidly.

The book that to this day attracts the most directors and producers

is *Cuckold.* It is an epic and has the potential for a period costume drama. It has an extremely unusual love triangle, wars, court intrigues, betrayals and, to top it all, a fifteenth-century princess who used to actually sing and dance in temples. It would certainly make a spectacular film even if you ignored the main thrust of the novel: the intensely introspective character of the male protagonist and his philosophical ruminations. One particular hot-shot director–producer team was in a desperate hurry. They even took me to Ooty for five days for a working session. The following year's Cannes festival was barely seventeen months away and I would have to convert my hefty novel into a screenplay within a month so that they could start shooting. I got down to work and never heard from these good people again.

There are various other walk-in characters like the lady lawyer of Indian origin from London who works for a multinational media giant and has been pursuing me for the last four years with one half-yearly email and telephone call assuring me that any moment now she will have concrete news for me. I like her, she doesn't give up and luckily I have no expectations. I guess the ruling principle of the world of cinema is hit-or-miss and you take your chances. I don't doubt that there must be a few good, honest souls in the industry. One of these days, who knows, I might run into one of them.

Black Tulip

I wrote the first version of *Black Tulip* between 2000 and 2001 with a few rewrites. And then I seem to have had a long bout of amnesia which lasted twelve years. Believe it or not, I had completely forgotten that I had written such a screenplay. Then sometime in 2013, I was sitting with my friend K.R. Harish, talking about movies, when it struck me that I had written a heist thriller a long time back. I had forgotten what I had called it and anyway I was sure that I had long since lost the manuscript. As it turned out, the original *Black Tulip* was still around. Harish read it and got hooked and encouraged me to work on it. I knew I would have to rewrite some of it but I had no idea how many times I would rewrite and re-re-re-revise the screenplay before I handed it over to my editors at HarperCollins.

Cops-and-robbers is a game that is, I suspect, common to most civilizations and cultures and of course it is one of the staples not merely in Hollywood and Bollywood but also in Hong Kong, France and wherever there's a film industry. But I was intrigued by a different wrinkle on the heist theme. Thieves and other varieties of crooks live in the same world as we do and like us they make political choices, read the same newspapers, watch movies, and share many of our stereotypes. They too must hate the red tape involved in getting a gas cylinder or having to warm the hands of innumerable clerks and officials to get a simple driving licence, not to mention giving 'hafta' to a policeman. We are familiar by now with even the highest police officers being on the take, often owning several flats and yet hanging on to official residences for decades long after they retire.

But let's take what most likely is the exception rather than the rule, the policewoman or man of integrity and honour. Which of us is so blasé that we will not respect and admire such a person? Imagine then a young, quick-fingered, big-time thief who hero-worships a policewoman. What you have on your hands in such a case is a complex character with all the contradictions and ambiguities which are the hallmark of us human beings. Rani is an unabashed fan of Additional Commissioner of Police, Regina Fielding. She has a Regina scrapbook and watches videos of her exploits. When Regina is posted back to Mumbai, Rani is delighted. She can now follow the policewoman in real time and even help her nab culprits by assisting her in oblique ways. At the same time she has her own life and her career or vocation to pursue. That should have posed an untenable dilemma for Rani since she knows that it is the ACP's duty to nab her. But the very real danger of getting caught merely adds an edge and spice to her exploits. Half the excitement, tension and fun for Rani lie in pitting herself against the policewoman she admires.

You get an inkling of how serious Rani is about her career in a brief scene where she is watching a heist film. What she sees on the screen is the standard set-up. The thief has made his peace with his life of crime and is living the quiet life of a retired gentleman when he's approached by an old friend who has a proposition for him: split six million dollars

right down the middle. All he wants of the one-time thief is one last job. And as is par for the course, the reformed thief insists that he's through with the past and won't take the job. At which point Rani scoffs at the cliché and speaks of an itch in the hands which is so compelling that it's exactly like any other addiction: you can't wean yourself off the habit and the excitement of pulling off one more job.

However, notwithstanding Rani's belief that 'once a thief, always a thief', she does of her own accord, though rather late in the day, hand herself over to ACP Regina Fielding. This happens when she learns that her whizkid boyfriend, Anzar, has gone missing. The young man has had to confront the question whether, as one of his employers has said, he's nothing but a techie-whore and will offer his services to the highest bidder. Anzar is forced to do some serious introspection and has a change of heart which will put his life at risk. What one is witnessing then is a journey of self-discovery for both Anzar and Rani. They belong to that generation which was born around 1991, a time when India did away with an avowed socialist vision for the country which, unfortunately, even then was observed more in the breach than in practice.

It is unsettling with what celerity we took to the free-market economy and its attendant loss of idealism, its self-absorption and its unfettered greed. The practice of this new theology demanded absolute adherence. You had no thought for anybody but yourself. The poor ceased to exist except that every cluster of high-rises demanded its own attached slum from where you recruited your cleaning woman, driver and the help who looked after your father who had so thoughtlessly picked up Alzheimer's.

Unlike their parents' generation, Anzar and Rani are not betraying any ideals. They are the 'now' generation unsullied by any fellow-feeling. In that sense, the two of them are remarkable. After the proverbial moment of truth, Anzar is willing to go the whole hog and make the ultimate sacrifice for the benefit of society. When Anzar goes missing as Rani and he are about to go on a holiday and she can't find him anywhere for days, she realizes that she has perhaps lost him forever. Her only hope is ACP Fielding. But Rani also knows that the

police officer will demand that she not only give up her career and ill-gotten wealth, but that she'll be sent to prison for several years. The choice is clear: it's either Anzar or her career and future. Once she has made up her mind she does not hesitate. She too will make the ultimate sacrifice to find Anzar, hopefully alive.

Black Tulip: A Screenplay with Two Endings

I've heard it said that very soon we will be able to choose our very own endings for movies. I'm afraid that has little appeal for me. Besides, I believe that the internal logic of a story must dictate the ending and not some whim either of the author or the viewer. But somewhere near the end of *Black Tulip*, I began to feel that either of two very different endings would fit integrally into the story. The first one ratcheted up the tension to the point that the whole city of Bombay is at grievous risk. You could call this particular version the one with an ultimately upbeat, 'happy ending'. There's no denying that commercial considerations dictate that Bollywood, not to mention, Hollywood, will more often than not opt for a contrived 'feel good' finis. But let's not forget that real life also does, at least occasionally, slip in an upbeat ending.

In truth, the postscript to this version of *Black Tulip* already had more than a germ of the second ending: it's reported on TV channels that a copycat heist has taken place in the mafia boss's own home. Instead of this occurring as nothing more than 'Breaking News', I decided to explore the elements of this new theft at some length. What I discovered though was that I would have betrayed the logic of the story if it ended at the point where the mafia boss got his comeuppance. No godfather worth his salt will allow anyone to damage his reputation without inflicting the most extreme punishment. Despite the 24/7 protection that Regina arranges for Rani, things go wrong, very wrong. In that sense, this is a much more disturbing closure to the screenplay. Moviemakers, if any such exist for *Black Tulip*, will have to choose the one they think works best. By and large, I've a feeling that they might opt for the ending that would be more popular. I would not view this

as a compromise. But right now, we don't have a movie. What we have is a screenplay in book form. So reader, you will have to pick the ending that you think is more germane to the story.

The Learning Curve

Perhaps you might grant that I'm not exactly a greenhorn when it comes to writing. Yet I will be the first to admit that working on *Black Tulip* has been a major learning experience. My first teacher was Ursula Koehler. As a former script-doctor, she was able to zero in on the weak points in *Black Tulip* almost instantly, but she's the soul of understatement and has the patience of a Redwood tree. She gave me many hints but the most valuable was to point out that I was not doing justice to the crisis and the consequent change in Rani's character when she is confronted with the loss of her boyfriend. My next major teacher was Michael Ott from the German Foreign Service who is an unrepentant film freak. I sent him *Black Tulip* on an impulse. It was he who suggested that it might be a good idea to stick to the film's central heist theme up to the end instead of merely touching upon it as a postscript.

I found my last advisor and guide through sheer serendipity. We had invited a couple over for dinner but they had a bit of a problem at the last minute. They had two guests staying with them. Well, we said, no problem, bring them along with you. They did. It was a lively evening. The unexpected male guest was a correspondent who had just finished a long stint in China and regaled us with scandals and murders in the Chinese bureaucratic hierarchy. As he and his wife were about to leave, it came to light that his wife, Tara Wilkinson, was a scriptwriter. To cut a not-so-long story short, she read the screenplay and made invaluable suggestions and taught me what the industry expects in terms of the presentation of a screenplay.

There was another kind of teacher, former Commissioner of Police Satish Sahney to whom I sent an earlier draft. Talk about monumental blundering, Satish Sahney will admit that I went beyond his worst expectations. I didn't even get the location of the head office of the

Mumbai Police right. Good, upright and helpful man that Sahney sahab is, he ploughed through the script, pointed out a mere 999 flaws and sent it back. I owe him a big thank you.

There was one other rather intriguing encounter with a person who taught me that human beings can be just as inaccessible as the fabled Fort Knox. This was the manager of a bank where I have had an account for over thirty years. I introduced myself to the lady and explained that I was an occasional novelist and wanted some information.

'What do you want to know?' she asked cagily.

I hemmed and hawed and said I wished to know which company the head office of the bank used for delivering cash to her branch and how was it delivered. Since I was aware that the information I was seeking was dubious, if not highly suspect, I asked her to check my bona fides: the fact that I was an old customer, that I really had written the occasional novel, that in recent memory I had not cheated the national exchequer of 73,000 billion dollars etc. That was it. Her eyes became slits from which she gave me the once-over, immediately called the security guard and asked him to keep a close watch on me while she disappeared into her cabin. I could see her through the glass wall. She was at her computer, checking the Internet. Fifteen minutes passed. I was convinced she had discovered the e-copy of my novel *Cuckold* and had got hooked. It was that kind of novel: so many people had told me that once you read the first paragraph, you couldn't stop till you reached the end at page 609.

Something was not quite right. She was making phone call after phone call. One of the bank employees opened the door of her office. 'I know when I see a crook,' I heard her say. 'Just send the police right away. I'll make sure he doesn't escape.' I waited for a police squad to arrive armed with semi-automatic guns, a public speaker system announcement that the building was surrounded, open fire and rush in, overpower and handcuff me and take me into custody. Another seventeen minutes later the manager reappeared. Fort Knox was definitely even more fortified now.

'No,' finally the Sphinx spoke. 'Because of your extremely advanced

age, you obviously don't know that times have changed. We don't deal in cash and nobody delivers money any longer. Everything's virtual now.'

'What nonsense,' I protested. 'I withdrew money just yesterday.'

She looked coldly at me. 'I suggest you leave right now because the police will be here any minute.'

I left meekly. A heavily armoured van with the initials CSM was waiting outside and two guards were removing sealed steel boxes from within.

Well, so much for the good teachers and the invaluable learning experience. But *Black Tulip* also offered some other not-so-happy but important lessons. Sometime last year I finally decided to try out a film agency. The revised version of *Black Tulip* had been cooking for quite a while and the basic story was fairly clear when I sent it to the agency. The response was dismissive and superior.

This was certainly not what I was expecting but at this stage of my career I have trained myself to understand that not only do viewpoints differ, radically at times, but that many a time the criticism may turn out to be valid and thus the author would be well-advised to take serious note of it. The agent's first query was: 'Why is Rani so interested in Regina Fielding and why would she follow her every move?' Any thief serious about his profession, I'd surmised, would naturally keep a watch on the police officer in charge of monetary crimes but I had also provided more than enough evidence of why Rani hero-worships the police officer and why she's in a sense stalking Regina.

His next question was even more baffling.

'But why does Rani steal?'

I had the strange feeling that the agent was in thrall of Bollywood and that too Bollywood of the 1980s when a man would be forced into a life of crime only to save his dying mother of cancer or to send his younger brother to medical school. That this is a likely scenario in our country is indisputable but the heist film is based on a different principle.

I must confess that I was thrown by this question since it's the

fundamental premise of the heist genre that one doesn't enquire deeply into why someone practises this particular profession. You don't need any psycho-babble or elaborate burrowing into the depths of the past or the protagonist's mind to zero in on the 'Big Why'. A brief exchange at the very end of Michael Crichton's novel and movie *The Great Train Robbery*, based on an actual heist and the trial that followed it, says it all:

JUDGE

[*Judgementally*]

Now, on the matter of motive, we ask you: Why did you conceive, plan and execute this dastardly and scandalous crime?

EDWARD PIERCE

I wanted the money.

I dropped the idea of hiring the film agency.

Isn't it ironic that no one asks why senior executives from Goldman Sachs, Morgan Stanley, Citibank and God knows how many other financial institutions who earn millions annually plus get monster bonuses, feel the need to swindle their own clients and pull off billion-dollar frauds? And are almost never punished for their crimes? So let us common folk lead our routine lives with our petty concerns and be grateful for heist movies which allow us to lead proxy lives through Rani and all those others who outsmart the cops and the system and give us vicarious thrills but, unlike the shameless CEO-cum-stupendous con artists, are ultimately corralled by the law.

When I started writing *Black Tulip*, I had hoped to write a carefree caper. But my characters took over and had their own ideas about where the story and the film should go. What the screenplay has turned out to be is darker at times. All I can say is that I hope you will enjoy *Black Tulip* and maybe, just maybe, we'll get to watch a terrific movie version of it.

Kiran Nagarkar
Mumbai, December 2014